More Praise of Renessa Boley

"So many of us get stuck in the career or business we thought we wanted only to find ourselves unfulfilled inside. Renessa's got the guide to plug you into your life's missions and pave the way to what you really want. I can't recommend her enough."

Barbara Niven
Hollywood's Top Media Trainer,
Actress and founder of Unleash Your Star Power

"It's clear from *Fast Lane, Wrong Direction* that Renessa just gets it. She's been in Corporate America. She's climbed the ladder. She gets it."

Stacy Kennedy
Founder, www.100Krealestate.com

"Renessa gave me the tools, the mindset and the strategies to evolve and thrive in a new working environment that I was completely unprepared for. Renessa brings clarity and she instills confidence. Anyone making a major professional transition needs a lot of both."

Phillip Druckenridge
U.S. government national security expert
(name pseudonymed for security purposes)

"Her poise, passion and fun personality made Renessa one of the most sought after speakers in the room. Renessa is an amazing leader who rocks any room she's in with love and optimism!"

Mary Agnes Antonopoulos
Coordinator, Christine's Comaford's 7-Figure Business Summit

FAST LANE
Wrong Direction

Insider Secrets to Redesign Your Success
and Reclaim Your Passion, Purpose
and Balance You Lost Along the Way.

RENESSA BOLEY

The Big! Life Network
Rockville, Maryland U.S.A.

Fast Lane, Wrong Direction
Insider Secrets to Redesign Your Success and Reclaim the Passion, Purpose and Balance You Lost Along the Way.

Copyright ©2013 Renessa Boley

ISBN-13: Softcover 978-1480297241
ISBN-10: Softcover 1480297240

Cover artwork copyright ©2013 by T.L. Price
Editing and composition by Dennis Tuttle, 5editorial, Silver Spring, Md.

All rights reserved. No part of this book may be reproduced or transmitted in any form or by any means, electronic or mechanical, including photocopying, recording, or by any information storage and retrieval system, without permission in writing from the copyright owner.

This book was printed in the United States of America.

10 9 8 7 6 5 4 3 2 1

For bulk or promotional copies of this book, contact:
www.fastlanewrongdirection.com

Also order this book online through:
www.amazon.com
www.barnesandnoble.com
www.fastlanewrongdirection.com
or from your favorite bookstore

*To Mommy and Daddy…
You saw me through my darkest days.
Because of you, I made it through.*

*To my future and my love, Aubrey…
You were right; life is about timing.
So delighted to be your bride!*

Contents

	Introduction	8
1.	How Did I Get Here?	16
2.	You Do Deserve More	22
3.	The Fraud Syndrome	28
4.	Coping Mechanisms	34
5.	Identity Theft	44
6.	The Need For Speed	50
7.	Nobody Does You Better Than You	56
8.	The Autobiography of Failure	62
9.	How to Get a High "Return on Failure"	70
10.	Busted Body	76
11.	It's All About Who You Know	82
12.	Fast Lane in Love	92
13.	It's Okay to Take a Pit Stop	100
14.	Listen to Your Life	110
15.	Stand Up For Your Life	116
16.	Forgiveness	124
17.	What Is Your Passion For Now?	130
18.	Intersection Between Passion and Marketplace	136
19.	Uncommon Sacrifices	144
20.	Uhh… You Need Help	152
21.	Dark Places	158
22.	It's Bigger Than You	166
23.	You Can Have Much More	178
	Acknowledgments	187

Sometimes you find yourself in the fast lane going in the wrong direction—in your career, in your business, even with the love of your life. In those moments, the last thing you need is motivation to keep going. In those moments… it's time to stop, look and listen to your life.

INTRODUCTION
• • • •
Slow Down So You Can Speed Up

WE ALL HAVE turning points in our lives, whether it's the trauma of getting fired, the heartbreak of divorce, the threat of a serious illness, losing a friend or suffering depression. For some of us, it's the inexplicable realization that we're bored out of our minds and scrambling for something—*anything!*—to pull us out of our funk.

For others, it's the chronic exhaustion that no amount of sleep can cure, or the irrepressible fear that somebody—*somewhere!*—will figure out we are a fraud. Still for others, it's as profoundly simple as catching a glimpse of ourselves in a mirror one day and wondering, "Who is that person?"

For me, it was all of the above, except getting fired and divorced, but a boss once suggested I consider another line of work. For a big ego chick like me, that rates pretty darn close to getting fired.

Whatever the turning point, that's when the questions begin…

The "how-the-hell-did-I-get-here?" questions.

No, seriously, how the hell did I get here?

Hitting that impasse in the road where you don't know where you're going and you don't know what to do (but you do know you're miserable) is a fairly common occurrence for many people—but not for the person who has it all together, zooming through life in the fast lane. Not for the person whom so many people admire and respect. This is not supposed to happen for the person who has worked, sacrificed and planned life so carefully, not for the person who has made the right decisions and taken the big risks. And certainly not for the person who looks, or is at least desperately trying to look, "the part."

Whether the impasse is supposed to happen to you or not is immaterial, because when it does, the reality of what's going on in your life vomits into your consciousness. You try to suppress it, but the truth of your relationships, your health, your emotional instability, your joy level or your fear keeps hurling itself back to the surface. It's a vivid metaphor, I know, but most of us are whizzing through life so completely numb that it takes a zinger to create any kind of real, emotionally honest reaction. Yet when we have that honest reaction to how things truly are in our lives instead of how we portray them on Facebook, that's when we're actually getting somewhere.

That's why I wrote this book.

My intention is to provide an insider's peek into the character, belief systems, ego and insecurities that keep some of us in well-dressed prisons, stuck in situations we hate and outright faking fulfillment. Whether you're squarely in the fast lane now or aspiring to shift into it, the goal of this book is to demonstrate how to soar in the fast lane while experiencing more passion and freedom to actually enjoy the ride. You may describe yourself as someone who has passed your "fast lane" prime, or maybe you question whether you've ever been in the fast lane at all. Regardless of your classification, if any of the opening sentences resonate with you, there is something for you in this book.

When I was a little girl, I wanted to be a news anchor, a fashion magazine editor, a Dallas Cowboys cheerleader and a Solid Gold Dancer. Yes — I've dated myself with the Solid Gold Dancer reference; don't judge me. But, somehow along the way, I got caught up in the chase to become an industrial engineer, a management consultant, a fast-rising "hypo" generating millions of dollars for a company, a real estate investor and some other interesting (and not so interesting) roles.

Through 15 years of climbing higher and higher, I trudged through life saying to myself (with a twinge of guilt), "There has got to be something more than this. I hate this—I really think I hate this." With successes and accolades, promise and potential, I developed digestive disorders, chronic fatigue, a mind and body that couldn't relax and a stack of "gratitude lists" for all the things I wanted to assure myself I was grateful to have.

I loved God, did a lot of good in the world, had a family that loved me and friends who accepted me, but at the core was a gnawing spirit of discontentment. I was so deliberate in applying to some of the "best" universities, making what I thought were the "right" choices, working for the "best" companies, yet as an old country song would say, "I was knee-deep in a river dying of thirst." With blessings enough to last two lifetimes, how could I feel like I got it so wrong?

Despite all my careful planning, my life was a mess. I say it was a mess because the quality of our lives is only a reflection of how we feel about it. Period. A lot of other people might weigh in, but how *we* feel about our lives is the only vote that counts.

And I felt like crap.

My problem: I was making a living, but I wasn't truly living my life. I was speeding along, making the best decisions I could in the moment, but never stopping to evaluate if the person I was becoming was who I wanted to be, or who I was designed to be.

I take that back....

I had a growing feeling from the time I was 17 years old that I was not becoming who I wanted to be. I was an engineering student interning for a technology company when my mentor asked what I wanted to do with my career.

I answered emphatically, "I want to work on a fashion magazine!"

His face reflected what I would say each day to myself: "Really, Renessa? And that's why you're working in a tech complex building file servers and inserting motherboards? Really?"

No.

The real reason was that engineering internship provided a full-tuition scholarship to Stanford University, a guaranteed internship each summer and a guaranteed post-graduation job. And if a company was willing to do all that for a military kid from a little Alabama town whose parents were barely 17 when she was born, then I would be anything they wanted me to be—gladly. That's why I was building file servers and inserting motherboards, and that's why the fashion magazine artwork was under the bed.

I was hopelessly bored on that job, and even then things deep inside felt a little off. But for a teenager making $11 an hour in 1993, they sure "looked" right! I couldn't articulate it at the time, but I had this fear my "right" decisions weren't going to turn out so right. It's kind of the same feeling we have when we pinpoint the first dude to die in a horror movie: We all know it's coming, but we have to let the scene play out. Deep down, I had this fear I would be successful, but not particularly happy.

In hindsight, I realize that experience conditioned me to always make decisions from a place of safety, from the perspective of what made logical sense and would protect me, whether that was personally, professionally, financially or otherwise. I had convinced myself my paycheck would make up for the boredom I felt in-between.

As I grew older, I effectively made the same "safe" decision on bigger scales with bigger consequences to my overall happiness. It was like hearing the click of the safety bar on a roller coaster; there's no getting off at that point. And my roller coaster had started up the track and was picking up speed. By my 20s, I was certainly in the fast lane going in the wrong direction, and all the while, I knew that whatever the destination, I was headed for an emotional train wreck.

But how do you explain having a really good life that you secretly don't want? Most people would say that's a you-don't-know-what-real-suffering-is kind of ingratitude.

So, instead of explaining, I decided to just quit. I quit the six-figure career. I quit the "rat race." It wasn't the first time I had walked away from a job, but this was different.

Instead of jumping into the next corporate gig, I took a timeout to look long and hard at the woman I had become.

What I realized is that I had been successful in many respects, but I never thought I was good enough. I was confident in what I could do, but I wasn't confident in who I was. There was so much insecurity, so much fear, and in the moments that I would admit the insecurity and fear, there was so much shame. I didn't admit the insecurity and fear too often because I had a reputation to protect; I'm sure you can understand. As a result, I ended up in the fast lane chasing opportunities I shouldn't have been chasing, clutching relationships that should have been released long before and failing to seize the joy, vitality and creativity that could have been mine all along.

Looking in the mirror and owning to my reflection was the scariest, most challenging, exhilarating and liberating experience, and it transformed me into the person I needed to become to strategically design my own success.

Strategically designing your success is not a privilege reserved for the lucky ones who get all the breaks, nor is it the prize you receive if you kick enough butt and take enough names. But it requires sacrifices unlike any that most are accustomed to making, including looking at your own reflection in the mirror and owning up to what you see. Unfortunately for the "fast-laner," when you bear the burden of the world's applause and all the ego trappings that accompany, you would just as soon let your life go down in flames than admit you've messed up and need a do-over.

I've found over the years the search for "right direction" is masked by law degrees, high heel shoes, busted relationships, briefcases, MAC makeup, loneliness, acrylic nails, MBAs, MDs, polo shirts, big bank accounts, mega debt, insecurity and regret—remnants of my fellow fast-laners who were just trying to keep it together, embarrassed to think they were the only ones who didn't know how to fix it and even more embarrassed to admit they don't quite know what "it" is, let alone how to fix it.

If that sounds like you, the good news is that you're not alone.

For this project, I interviewed many people from different backgrounds, countries and industries—men, women, single, married, kids, no kids, careerists and entrepreneurs. Some were millionaires, others were rebuilding from a financial setback.

Regardless of the circumstances, the similarities were startling:

• "You may not even like the person you've become, but the success has become a drug. The person who's crying at night, the person who numbs themselves with wine... that's the real person with the real pain. The true you and the you that you want us to see are very different."

— *Johnny, investor*

- "I was working on a project for a year. I tore a ligament in my knee and needed surgery, but I couldn't do it. I told myself, 'I can't afford to not be chargeable.' I worked through the pain. I didn't take the physical therapy. When I did, it took me three months to heal instead of the initial three weeks. Psychologically and emotionally, I think it took me three months because my body didn't want to go back. My body literally didn't heal. I was burned out."

— *Teresa, business consulting manager*

- "I would get there at 7 o'clock, thinking that if I put in 12 or 14 hours, I would have stuff done and would have everything under control. Leaving the office at 9, 10 or 11 o'clock at night, I never felt a hundred percent confident about my day's work. I never felt accomplished enough, that I handled the situations the right way. Nothing was ever good enough, not because someone told me I wasn't good enough but because in my head I thought I wasn't good enough."

— *Cameron, marketing director*

- "Had I gone to a top law school, I could've written my own check. If I was around people who went to top law schools, I felt inadequate. The lack of confidence was so loud."

— *Kennedy, attorney*

- "People see what someone else is presenting as 'this only took me six months to do.' If you don't do it in six months, you've failed. If you don't do this in 12 months, you're not meant to be a businessperson. If you don't do this in 18 months, you should go back to Corporate America because you can't hack it. It goes back to somebody else's internal sense of failure."

— *Samantha, entrepreneur*

- "Nothing is ever enough; the focus is on the next big thing. When you hit it, there's no time to celebrate; it's on to the next big deal! I'm not only that way at work. I didn't go to my grad school graduation; it wasn't a big deal to me. I marvel at people who are genuinely able to celebrate things."

— *Tabitha, entrepreneur*

- "There's this belief that you can't show any weakness. You can't show that you don't know something or you don't have the answer. There's this perception that if I show that, they won't have as much faith and confidence in me. They won't hire me. They won't let me be in charge of the project. So even if I don't know, I'd better act like I know it."

— *Paul, business owner*

As you can see, "fast lane, wrong direction" is not necessarily about being in the wrong career. To be clear, this book is a not a rant against Corporate America, as any business owner will tell you entrepreneurship comes with unimaginable stresses of its own. The point is that we can have that dream job or business, but the fear, competition, anxiety and insecurity we may display in the pursuit of our goals can become a disaster in the other areas of life that matter to us.

So, how does an achiever write a book for achievers? It's no easy task, because even with all my own personal growth, everything in me was afraid of being judged—from the book cover to the internal formatting to the length of the book. "Is it too long? Is it too short? What will people think? Will they find value? Is it too wordy? So and so says I'm wordy."

But since I have to walk my talk with everything I do, the only thing I could do was apply the very principles I share in the book as I write the book. The very fact you are reading right now is proof that the perfectionist in me, the part that is committed to finding yet another reason why the book isn't "just right," lost out to the woman who values herself enough to say, "Good enough is good enough. Get this book out there and help somebody!"

In *Fast Lane, Wrong Direction,* you'll be challenged with some tough questions to which there are no universal "right" answers, yet all the answers have consequences.

You'll see what "fast lane, *right* direction" looks like for some people, how that relates to you and what you should expect as you make the small and radical changes to merely shift lanes or change direction altogether. The voices in your head, the insecurities, the confidence everybody thinks you have but you fear you don't… I've got you. By the end of this book, I hope you will get real about where you are, where you want to be and whom you need to become in order to create a life you are proud to call your own.

"How did things get so off-track and I didn't notice?"
— Priya, attorney

CHAPTER 1
••••
How Did I Get Here?

VERY MUCH LIKE Alcoholics Anonymous, the first step in making any major change is admitting there is a problem. I don't mean admitting a universal problem of success without fulfillment. I mean admitting you have a problem and you are unfulfilled.

Many of us are afraid to look inside and take honest assessment of where we are because we have become so invested in our direction, whatever that direction happens to be. It could be the money and time invested in advanced education. It could be the years dedicated to practice with little or no pay. It could be all the dreams and desires deferred until you "made it." Whatever the investment, if we realize we are going in the wrong direction, we often have no freakin' clue what we're supposed to do next, and that scares the you-know-what out of us.

When I was entering college as an engineering student, a mentor advised me, "Just sacrifice seven years and then it will get better. Seven years and it will be all worth it."

That was the best and absolute worst advice I had ever received—best because it equipped me to endure some of the sucky years early in my career, which, in truth, is what we all have to endure on the road to success. But it was the worst because it was incomplete advice and, as a result, I abdicated the inner compass that signaled when I was off-track, when something just didn't feel right.

In some instances, that inner compass tells us when we need to make a slight lane shift; other times it's a big red flashing light signaling us to STOP, back up and hightail it out of there as fast as we possibly can. I didn't understand any of the signals at the time. I was in that "no-pain, no-gain" career frame of mind. The more pain I endured, the better I thought it would be on the other side.

So, how do we end up in the wrong direction in the first place? For Rochelle, it was completely by design...

"THERE WAS a period in my life when I felt I was definitely in the wrong direction, and the funny part of it is I was there on purpose; I was there by design. I had left my previous company and just finished business school. I wanted to do traditional management consulting and I knew I wanted to do it in the human resources space because that's what I enjoy—HR organizational development. There are a few companies that are experts in this field so I specifically targeted them. I made some connections through my network and within two months had a job with one of the top HR consulting firms. It was exactly what I wanted to do...

...and it was the devil's den.

I hated every minute of it. It was a disaster! I hated the work. I hated the person running the practice where I worked. I hated how work made me feel.

It's funny because I was probably in the best physical condition of my life during that two-year term. The office was across the street from my sports club, and when I'd reach the point where I just couldn't take it anymore, I would run from the office for the gym, screaming. I was at the gym two or three times a day —any break I'd have in my schedule. For some reason, when I was in the office building, I would get headaches. I would feel like I was going to faint, like I was literally having a physical reaction to how wrong a situation I had put myself in. It was a nightmare.

I would go home from work every evening almost in tears. The weekend, especially Friday, was such a relief, but the Sunday blues would start around 3 o'clock in the afternoon, and I would start getting depressed. By 9 o'clock Sunday night, I would be in tears again. It was so horrible. It was the epitome of 'be careful what you wish for you because you just might get it.'**"**

A scenario such as Rochelle's plagues so many people I encounter and coach, and it creates an incredible amount of guilt for people because their living hell is wholly self-inflicted and completely deliberate. There's a real-life feeling of the old cliché that since they made their bed, they must now lie in it. But that couldn't be farther from the truth, as you'll soon learn. For Jacob, wrong direction came as an unexpected twist of life...

"I STARTED OFF doing exactly what I wanted to do, which was playing in a band. When I was 18 or 19 years old, I landed this role on Australian television, I was jumping out of airplanes and doing all sorts of fun stuff. I started getting a degree in real estate economics in order to satisfy my parents and to make sure I always had a trade to go back to. That's what they always wanted me to do. After graduating, I started working with one of Australia's biggest real estate companies as a property evaluator. So I was 23 years old with this huge glass office in this big company.

All of sudden, my family hit bottom. My father was being sued by his franchise owners for a couple of million dollars and the tax people were after him, as well. I was put in the position to help my family survive. We lost our family home, all the boats and toys… everything! We lost our feeling of significance as a family because we had a belief that we were only valuable if we were wealthy and prominent.

The first few years were really tough and I worked every day as hard as I could to create money because that is what I perceived to be of personal significance. I started smoking marijuana and drinking, and the pace affected my health badly because I didn't know how to relieve the day-to-day pressure. I didn't have any friends other than people I respected in business; that's all I really had time for. I didn't have the emotional energy for deeper connection, so I only dated women who were more like friends. From the spiritual point of view, there was none of that. I did not believe in God because… how the hell could this happen to me if there was God? I saw myself as a victim, through and through.

I just wanted to escape from living in our terrible rented house, which is all my parents and I could afford at the time. Banks would not give us a loan, but through a process of trial and error, I got the business on track. Yet, ironically, I was always struggling for cash because I had all these people to pay.

There was a feeling of being detached and numb, where you just kind of work every day and you don't really know why and nothing feels real. And I would do stupid things. I remember during this period that I just wanted to feel something. One day I was riding in a cab with a friend and I just decided I was going to jump out of the car. And so I opened the door and just jumped out of this cab running 60 kilometers an hour… I just jumped out! I… I didn't roll or anything. I just hit the ground with a thud.

As I looked up, it was one of the first moments of a wake-up call for me because I was so wounded I could not breathe. I just lay there as my head hit the ground really hard. I was defenseless. I had this feeling of how fragile I was for the very first time. I realized at some level I had caused that pain and kind of linked in my mind that I had caused the other pain in my life, as well. I realized I was making some pretty bad decisions.

Perhaps I should state the obvious here. From the outside, Jacob and his family had it pretty good. But the point of Jacob's pain is that life happens, right? And things aren't always as they appear. You can be sailing along, and *wham!* Like Jacob, you find yourself so far off-track you don't know which decision derailed you.

What makes new entrepreneurs so vulnerable to wrong direction is most have just a glimpse of what they want to build through their business. They tend to have a sketchy idea of a future outcome and an even sketchier plan for how to make it reality. To close the gap, they start gathering resources, attending seminars, reading books and listening to the advice of market gurus—all to find the fastest way to success. I call it the "Copycat Effect."

Wrong direction occurs not because of the resources, seminars, books or advice. It occurs because of a lack of clarity about their business at the core and its intrinsic value to the marketplace, regardless of the business being a boom or bust. As a result, many have a hard time distinguishing when they are making the right choices for their business versus merely copying the vision, strategy and activity of some mentor or guru. Diana recalled her early entrepreneurial experience this way:

"WHEN YOU FIRST start, you've put your money or someone else's money into these things and you want to see a return on it. You're hard-charging and plugging away, and all you want to do is get to this place where you've made it. So you're diverting your funds into things you don't need to do. I might not need to speak on stage or be on CNN or have an online site. You start doing all these things that may not necessarily align with your original purpose because someone told you that's what you should do to make it—and make it fast.

There are the base things you should do for your particular business, and most people don't take the time to do the base things. I didn't. So we're moving fast, but we don't know where we're going. We've spread ourselves too thin, and we're totally in the wrong direction because we're following the advice of these people who have 'made it.'"

Following the advice of people who have "made it" makes a lot more sense than following the advice of those who haven't! But you can be doing all the "right" things yet unwittingly have the wrong vision, and that will yield wrong-direction results. I can't think of one entrepreneur who hasn't gone down that road a time or two.

When I was younger, I believed I was smart enough to accomplish anything, but my concept of "anything" was so limited. I could be a doctor, a lawyer, a journalist or an engineer... that was about as broad as it got for me. The "Solid Gold" show I mentioned in the introduction was off the air by then, so the dancer option was a no-go. When the college recruiters came knocking for more women and underrepresented groups in math- and science-based fields, I was all-in. I went with the tide because, like so many others, I didn't know anything different.

So the common question we ask ourselves is: What could we have done differently? Oftentimes, we revisit some of our boneheaded decisions and clearly understand what could have been done differently. Other times, there is no "different" decision; we made the best decisions we could with the resources we had, and we recognize those experi-

Conversations in the Fast Lane

✓ If there is a "wrong direction" in any area of your life, how did you get there? Was it by accident, by design or unexpected circumstance?

✓ Have you at any point been afraid to take an honest assessment of who you are and what you truly want? If so, why?

✓ Do you acknowledge any ways in which your "wrong direction" has been self-inflicted?

✓ Has some minor irritation in your life somehow ballooned into something more?

✓ What do you want to do now?

---

ences refined us into the people we are today.

It doesn't really matter how you ended up in a wrong direction, whether it was by accident or completely by design. Perhaps the better question—and the harder question—is what do you do now? When it comes to career, it is sometimes comfortable to stay in what some call the "rat race" because at least there are other people there keeping you company.

There is a tremendous amount of fear when considering the kind of change that would impact your income, image, perceived security or your family. When you are single with no responsibilities, you only have to worry about the impact that change will have on you, and that's a burden in itself. But when you have other people who depend on you, you must consider the impact the life-changing disruption will have on them, real or imagined.

Whether you're afraid of changing cities, leaving a relationship or the impact a more flexible work schedule will have on your perception of office "face time," you must also consider the cost of staying in the wrong direction. What happens if you don't figure this out? You may think these emotions will dissipate over time, or that your status or financial security or lifestyle will make up for the burgeoning discontentment in your heart.

Let's be clear: what might start out as a minor irritation may inevitably balloon uncontrollably if ignored. No amount of willpower, discipline or emotional mastery will stop the Mount Vesuvius that's waiting to erupt in your life. The only difference between one "fast lane, wrong direction" and another is how long the person holds out and suffers. There are no medals for suffering unnecessarily, and you deserve so much more than that.

"I push myself. I go for it. I'm up early,
I stay up late. I'm going after my dreams.
These are things that need to be applauded."
— Roberto, politician

CHAPTER 2
• • • •
You Do Deserve More

AMBITION. RESOURCEFULNESS. FOCUS. Positivity. Willingness to take risks. Going for it. Service. Inspiration. Passion. Faith. Creativity. Pushing yourself. Pure, unadulterated balls. Charisma. Leadership. Initiative. Vision. Follow-through. Innovation. Generosity. Execution. Reliability. Organization. Integrity. Guts. Sacrifice. Courage.

Those are just some of the reasons fast-laners are simply awesome! We carry an uncanny desire to contribute to the world and make it a more dynamic place. Sometimes those dreams go hand-in-hand with a vision of our name in lights on billboards along the highway, but this section is not about egotistic flaws. This section is about our awesomeness.

We are the leaders, the dynamic ones and the risk-takers. We take no prisoners—of ourselves or others—and often there is no room for weakness. Second place is first loser, so get out of our way cause we're coming through!

We live our lives at a very high standard. The purpose of that standard is often to give back to the people and causes we value, and we need to use every ounce of what we have to its highest potential. So, when a parent or close friend is in need, they go to the one they know will get it done—you. And that's a good thing. That's a very good thing.

Notice on the list of laurels at the beginning of the chapter that you don't see the word "happy." Because for a lot of fast-laners, all the accomplishments don't produce happiness, and the dilemma for many achievers is they feel they have no right to be unhappy or discontented or frustrated or depressed because they are ambitious, resourceful, dynamic and all the other things on the why-I'm-so-awesome list.

> "Who do I think I am? Why should I be miserable?
> I have a good life. Why should I want more?"
> — *Cassandra, public relations vice president*

It's Cassandra's kind of thinking that has people stuck in situations they hate, suffering unnecessarily because of an internal or external perception that they already have enough in life. You do have enough of a lot of things, but perhaps not enough of the things that matter, fulfill, satisfy or quench the thirst of your spirit. Everyone is entitled to these things, whether you are a fast-laner or a "Joe Six Pack."

In order to get more of that passion, purpose and balance to enjoy your success, it is important to first reject the notion that you don't deserve it or that a finite amount of feel-good blessings have been doled out and you have received more than your fair share. Remember: the quality of your life is a reflection of how you feel about it. And if you feel as if you want more, different or better, maybe there's something to that, too.

Please don't misunderstand me when I say this. Clearly, we must have gratitude for the very air we breathe, the fact that our hearts beat in the middle of the night, for all those things that work on our behalf over which we have no control.

Gratitude is huge.

The problem happens when people use gratitude as an excuse to not step up—to avoid making major decisions in life or stepping out on faith to get what they *really* want, not what they've been conditioned to want over the years. If something is clearly not working in your life, maybe you are not happy in your business; maybe you haven't been for years. Maybe you need to make a shift in your life and it's been rubbing you raw. Those are signals that something needs to change.

Your emotions are a gift. They often indicate when to move, when to stop, when to change, when to stay, when something is right and when something is wrong. But most of us view emotions as something to be controlled, subdued and mastered. Obviously, there's a time and place to act on our emotions, but our emotions are our GPS.

You know by now the definition of success is not just making a lot of money. For me, true success is massive achievement combined with being completely fired up on all cylinders—in your health, finances, relationships and faith.

But some people who are wildly successful in their career or business hate getting out of bed and hate going to their job. They are fighting against life for eight to 10 hours of the day, overworked and dejected. That signal is not going to go away; it's only going to get louder and louder. It's going to create stress until they change. But the pain is actually serving as a gift because it's causing a response. More times than not, people only make major changes in their life in response to pain.

Think about it. You may not go to a dentist for a regular checkup, but when your tooth hurts badly enough, you speed-race to that appointment. Consider the last major shift you had in your life. Maybe it was a breakup. Maybe you ended a friendship. Maybe you left a company. You probably couldn't take it anymore. You were so aggravated, you were so fed up, you were so... *something!*

So I'm talking to those of you who mumble about missing out on life, the ones who grumble about the working conditions or the hours or the lack of freedom you have. That's a signal. Corporate America is never going to change because its business model has worked just fine for decades.

It is not the responsibility of your boss to create opportunities for your fulfillment. It is not your business or your company's fault you've turned into a monster of a person to be around, even though other monsters in the workplace may surround you. It's on *you* to look deep inside, read the tea leaves to get it, decide what *you* want and have the courage to become who *you* need to be.

Successful people follow their gut—that ever-still inner voice that rises when we do or do not want to do something. It's our internal compass. People often underestimate the gift of emotion and gift of intuition, and instead hold out in situations far longer than they should, waiting for some "miraculous sign" when losing 10 pounds or gaining 10 pounds or having insomnia or being consistently sick should be all the sign they need.

Sometimes, how your emotions respond is completely contrary to what logic is telling you. But passion speaks louder than logic. It may be telling you to go in one direction, to pursue a dream, to make a move, to change a life circumstance, yet your head is screaming, "You've got to be kidding me?! How in the world am I going to do that?"

If you snuff out that flame with the excuse that you just need to be content with what you have, you'll never experience the level of fulfillment you're capable of achieving. Or you'll hit material success yet miss the whole joy of living. As you may already know, there are few things more disillusioning than making it big only to get to the top and discover the climb wasn't worth it.

Over lunch, my friend Tracy said something that deeply resonated with me:

> **"THERE ARE PERIODS** of my life I totally don't remember. I was zooming so fast from one achievement to another that there are chunks of time when I don't remember what happened in between. My father would remind me of people or events from time to time that I would have no recollection of. I was once in an airport and bumped into an old high school classmate. He was so excited to reconnect, so we talked briefly. The sad thing is I had no idea who he was."

I could relate to Tracy because my own momma used to say to me, "You don't remember anything!"

> **Conversations in the Fast Lane**
>
> ✓ When you recall the list of adjectives that describe who you are, how often do the words "happy" or "fulfilled" apply?
>
> ✓ Do you ever feel as if you have no "right" to be unhappy or discontent or frustrated?
>
> ✓ Do you ever feel an internal conflict between being content with your life and desiring more from it?
>
> ✓ If yes, how has that conflict affected what you have done (or haven't done) to change your circumstances?
>
> ✓ Do you tend to shut down your emotions or overreact to them? Do you know how to appropriately read your emotions and what they're revealing to you?

• •

"Not true," I thought.

I still remember that A+ I got on my CS106A computer science program my sophomore year in college. It was one of the hardest things I ever did, and I still think I have a memorial to that feat in a chest of old keepsakes. But I can't vividly remember one movie night hanging out in my college dorm, so I guess I missed the point.

I missed the moments.

So what does all of that mean for you?

1.) It means to appreciate everything that has shown up in your life to date, however you got here, and be grateful. This will serve you moving forward;

2.) It means noticing where you're experiencing pain in the form of boredom, discontentment, frustration, aggravation or loneliness because that is a signal to change, to move in a new direction. That may not necessarily mean quitting your job, changing businesses or walking away from a commitment, but it may mean that you change some aspect of what you are doing. For me, I needed to change directions altogether, so I up-and-quit. I lived from my head and not my heart for nearly 15 years, and though I was consistently promoted and advanced, my health suffered tremendously. I battled with low-grade depression, and I spent most days on autopilot. Beyond the money, that was nowhere near true success;

3.) While you are not to be driven solely by emotion, you must make a decision to no longer mask the emotions or suppress them. Instead, use them as a guide to your own personal map for success. The path to success is not easy and doesn't feel good all the time, but you will know in your spirit, in your heart and intuition, if what you are doing is not in line with what you want. That is a very important key to true success.

So the question is: Do you know how to read your emotions and what they are telling you about your life? Can you distinguish between when they are leading you to do something reckless and destructive or when they are your guides from on high?

> "In public, we were this awesome couple. He was handsome; I was beautiful. We had great kids between us. He was awesome. . . No, it was not. He was not happy I was getting attention or the amount of time I was putting into the business. In public, we were this awesome couple; in private we were crumbling."
> — *Patsy, entrepreneur*

You deserve more than just acting the part as Patsy did; you deserve to be the part. You deserve more. Not more accolades and trophies and standing ovations. I'm talking about more life, more laughter, more connection, more love, more passion, more energy, more depth, more substance because that's what makes the accolades and trophies and standing O's meaningful.

You deserve more moments.

Here's a little secret…
None of your talent, resources, connections
or achievements will ever satisfy until you come
to grips with a bona fide truth:
If you never possessed any of your talent, resources,
connections or achievements, you'd still be
the fiercest fox to ever rock the spot.
You, alone, are enough.

CHAPTER 3
....
The Fraud Syndrome

BELIEVE IT OR not, all of our fears (the non-life and death ones, anyway) boil down to two simple root questions: 1.) Will I be loved? 2.) Am I enough?

If you trace every fear you've had of doing most anything, whether it was stepping up to a gorgeous woman on the street, opening your heart to a new relationship or going for that promotion, the fear was likely rooted in one of those two questions. If you try to explain every crazy, destructive or counterproductive behavior you've ever displayed, it would be rooted in one or both of those questions. How attached you are to the answer of those questions will dictate how far out on a limb you're willing to go on the one hand, and how irrationally foolish you're willing to be on the other.

The irony is the answer to those questions, always, is a resounding *yes!* That doesn't mean you're always right (ask former President George W. Bush), nor does it mean you're always best-suited for your particular pursuit (Michael Jordan trying baseball), nor does it mean everyone will applaud you (read any celebrity magazine), but it doesn't make the statement any less true.

You are loved—always. And you are enough—always, whether or not anyone ever agrees with you.

Before you start dismissing this as "woo-woo" psychobabble, consider how profound and truthful this realization is for a lot of people. Most of us have never been taught to view ourselves as innately worthy; instead, we've been taught to seek validation. Our value and achievements are disproportionately influenced by how other people view us. We seek validation from our teachers, parents, friends, spouse, customers and boss. We're fiending for someone to praise and validate our job well done. We make a funny comment on Facebook, and we're disappointed if it doesn't get as many "likes" or LOLs as we expect. Our need for validation influences nearly every aspect of our lives.

A hugely successful real estate investor told me something that really hit home:

"Put us on the stage and we'll perform, but sit us down by ourselves and ask us if we believe we're as good as they say we are, and we're in trouble."

If someone were to ask if you were confident, you would likely say, "Yes." Even if you didn't actually believe it, you would think the person asking expected you to be confident, so you would be an idiot to say, "No." But I challenge you on why you believe yourself to be confident, if you indeed do. Are you confident because of what you have done and what you have accomplished, or are you confident because of who you *are*?

You would be amazed how prevalent low self-esteem is for the people I have interviewed. It took on many forms, but the fear of not being loved and the failure to realize they already were enough motivated people to achieve the heights of accomplishments in sometimes the most destructive ways. No amount of achievement will satisfy you until you realize the value of who you are. If your self-worth is tied to your net worth, or your opinion of yourself is a function of your perceived stock value in the marketplace of public opinion, you may likely be experiencing what I call the "Fraud Syndrome."

I was fairly proud of myself and thought this was quite the innovative term until I realized it was wholly unoriginal; I think "The Fraud Syndrome" was coined in 1978.

That sucked.

Then I asked myself how could I put an innovative spin on the term so people wouldn't think I copied the concept. The 10 minutes I spent debating myself about keeping or changing the title of this chapter is only more evidence that all of our fears come down to those two big questions at the beginning . While I have gotten 110 percent better over the years, I'm clearly still guilty of my own ego trips.

I don't know what other "experts" have to say about the Fraud Syndrome; all I know is how it presented itself in my life, the lives of countless people I've coached over the years and in nearly every person I interviewed. It's this idea that you're never quite good enough, and, at any moment, somebody is going to discover you really don't deserve all those kudos, that you're really a mess inside, barely keeping it together. Somebody is going to find out you're a fake. One of my coaching clients described it perfectly:

"The desire to be special and different was exacerbated at the firm. When I became a regular fish surrounded by so many other smart people, I felt like a phony. I really didn't belong and eventually they would find out."

Wow. This woman graduated Yale undergrad and Georgetown Law School. By all external accounts, she was hot stuff. When we met, she was working for one of the premier law firms in the country, yet she didn't feel as if she belonged. We worked together as she transitioned out of law to start her own real estate investment company, something she is tremendously passionate about. She confessed some time later:

"Maybe I should have made partner just to prove I could have. There's something in me that feels bad for not being the best. Then there's a part of me that says, 'Yeah, you should have left because you weren't really good enough.'"

That is the classic case of the Fraud Syndrome. I have experienced it many times before and with so many people I have coached. No matter how good you are, in your mind you're never good *enough,* and that's assuming all is well in your world. When all is not well and you are in a season of failure or disappointment, all hell often breaks loose in your mind.

The Fraud Syndrome manifests itself in two distinct ways: as insecurity (or a lack of confidence) and as an insatiable need for external validation.

Insecurity and Lack of Confidence

Insecurity played out in my own life in a way I would have never expected. Several years ago, I started investing in residential real estate. It was my first go at financial freedom, and I started investing in properties left and right with a business partner. It was a successful run in many respects and a total debacle in others. The relationship started out exciting and over time disintegrated into the partnership from hell. Out of respect for the other party and the fact there are always two sides to every story, I'll omit the details, but I will share what that experience revealed about me.

I should have ended the partnership two years before it actually fell apart. I was unhappy, felt disrespected and came to really dislike my partner. But at my core I felt as if I couldn't accomplish the big dreams I had for the business without her abilities, so I endured a very unhealthy dynamic to keep the dreams alive. I was the primary financier for the business, and I certainly brought skills to the table, but I was a grasshopper in my own eyes. She was more assertive, more aggressive and quick on her feet.

In hindsight, I realize that some of her qualities weren't necessarily the most endearing, but at the time I thought I *needed* her partnership to be successful. She was definitely a very talented woman and an asset to any team, and I'm a firm believer that when choosing to partner with someone, they should bring skills that you lack. Otherwise, why partner? But you never need anyone at the expense of your own happiness, and that's where I tripped.

We had a fair business partnership for the most part, and I think we both generally made decisions that were in the best interest of the business, but the interpersonal dynamic sucked because I didn't have confidence in my own value. As a result, I allowed her to run over me emotionally. I was too insecure to take a stand for how I should have been treated. I thought I was enduring the discomfort and resentment for the sake of the business when, in actuality, it was because I didn't believe I was good enough to succeed without her.

When you are driven by ego, whether in the form of insecurity as I was or external validation, you can be manipulated to do anything. I reflect on that season of my life and think, "What the [bleep]?!" I would have never thought in a million years that I would have allowed someone to treat me that way, but because I couldn't fully appreciate my own value at the time, I did.

Insecurity and risk-taking go beyond the career and business arena. Jillian is a brilliant and dynamic chief operating officer for a company, yet she confided:

> *I* DON'T FEEL like I have a lot to offer to a partner. I'm unhappy and unfulfilled. I wouldn't date me, so I give my number to people I would never date. I get hit on by 20-somethings and I give my number to them because I have less of a shot of disappointing them. To the 40-year-old who's got it together, I'm not together, and I don't want to date someone who could judge me.

Accomplishments may mask the fact that driven people have self-esteem issues, but as evidenced by these stories, the truth will surface one way or another.

The Need For Validation

The need for validation is a close cousin to insecurity. People who need validation will get cranking, but only after they have the green light that they are going in the right direction through the approval of others. Remember, when your ego is influenced by the praise or criticism of other people, you can be manipulated to do absolutely anything. Most people don't realize this until it's too late.

Janet ended up in a situation where she allowed a superior to sexually harass her for two years. She feared it would compromise all she had worked to achieve if she came forward about the abuse of power. Janet is quite advanced within her organization and had once been tapped for a chief information officer position within a federal agency. Why did she tolerate the abuse for so long?

"I no longer considered myself important. I no longer valued Janet," she said. "The money, status and title were more important. It's sad when you think about it. The reason it went on so long was because I was determined to endure it to get to the next level. And it shocked everybody. Every single person in my relationship spectrum was shocked and devastated. No one would have ever imagined that would happen to someone like me."

When we lose ourselves in pursuit of something external that we have linked to our self-worth, we can end up in the midst of inexplicable circumstances with no idea how we allowed it to happen. For Janet, the money, status and title validated who she was to the extent that she lost sight of the fact she was worth more than she was tolerating.

> ## Conversations in the Fast Lane
>
> ✓ When you trace back your fears or evaluate any counterproductive behavior, do you find it rooted in these two main questions: "Will I be loved?" and "Am I enough?"
>
> ✓ In your past, did you generally believe you were intrinsically worthy or did you seek to be validated?
>
> ✓ How does the "Fraud Syndrome" manifest in your life, if at all?
>
> ✓ When driven by ego, we can be manipulated to do anything. Have you been manipulated in any way by the chase of external validation?
>
> ✓ Have you ever been at the mercy of somebody else's ego trip?

Don't think that applies to you?

Well, consider a situation in your life where you look back and wonder, "How did I let that happen to me?" Or those moments where you thought, "Oh, no, she didn't!" (complete with eye roll and attitude).

But, yeah… she did. Or maybe *he* did. Either way, no matter how painful, uncomfortable or complicated the circumstances, you must investigate whether or not, on some level, you allowed it happen.

How?

Because you put yourself at the mercy of somebody else's ego trip. It could be you maintained a relationship far longer than you should have, like I did. Maybe you still allow yourself to be manipulated by people in your family. Perhaps you have done something on the job for professional gain that you regret.

The reality of this topic is a hard one for most achievers, but it is so crucial because it is the driving force behind our unhappiness. The good news is there are a few things you can do now so your value is never again contingent on the validation of someone else.

Do not misunderstand; I am by no means suggesting other people's input or evaluation of you is unimportant. For instance, people's perspective on this book may influence the writing of the next one. If I hear crickets in the audience as reaction to a motivational point instead of the expected chuckles, it is a sure sign that point won't make the cut in the next speech.

But no feedback, good or bad, has any bearing on my worth. Likewise, that I failed somewhere along the way, that I didn't know the answer or that I still haven't figured it all out doesn't make me any more or less valuable, although in somebody else's eyes I might be less valued. That's called their problem, not mine, and the same holds true for you.

"Fast Lane, *Right* Direction"
is developed when you're strong enough
to look at yourself—the good, the bad, the ugly—
and embrace that you are enough.

CHAPTER 4
••••
Coping Mechanisms

WE ALL HAVE coping mechanisms to deal with life's discomforts, whether it is food, alcohol, sex, whatever. If you ever want the courage to begin making decisions that align with your happiness, the first step is to recognize that your current coping mechanisms just aren't working.

My friends know I have a white cheddar popcorn fetish, and on a bad day, I'll make a quick trip to the local Trader Joe's market and down an entire bag in one sitting. I know in my mind this is a bad idea, but in the moment, that one blissful hour of escape is worth the dairy hangover the next morning. The coping mechanisms I'm talking about, though, have more far-reaching effects than white cheddar popcorn, and it's time to see them for what they are.

Earlier in Chapter 1, we heard Jacob discuss feeling numb and detached, as if nothing felt real. The numbness is actually what allows people to keep moving forward without changing direction, to avoid the very situations they need to face. It's a coping mechanism, but that state of numbness should create high alarm because it is actually the most dangerous place to be.

In the stages of hypothermia, you know the first stage is uncontrollable shivering due to the cold. But over time, the extremities begin to go numb and the person actually stops feeling cold. They feel less discomfort, yet they are actually dangerously close to freezing to death.

That is eerily similar to what happens when you are going in the wrong direction.

If you truly *feel* what you feel—the guilt, disappointment or fear in your situation—then you are forced to react and do something about it. You can't ignore the pain any more than you can withstand freezing temperatures without shivering. In those instances, some people do the hard work of confronting where they are versus where they truly want to be and decide to take action. Most, however, go numb to escape because feeling nothing is easier than facing the issues.

There are three particularly destructive coping mechanisms people use to go numb, and they're destructive because just like the latter stages of hypothermia, we actually feel better about ourselves in the moment. In those moments, however, we fail to realize how much more damage we are piling on to an already dangerous situation.

The Butthole Syndrome

I'm sure you can think of a more apropos title for this section, but I decided to keep it clean. Here's what Angela says about her bout with "The Butthole Syndrome" in her last job:

"I was irritable, but I was rewarded for that. 'Watch out for Angela!' they would say. I left a lot of bodies along the way and I humiliated people. It was a power and control thing. Between the pressure of the job, being unhappy and being immature, I took on the pit bull mentality. I was always being grilled about my credentials, so I was already on the defensive. It boiled down to fear."

It happens all the time. People want to kick butt and take names because that's what they think it takes to earn respect and make it to the top. Angela had it right when she said it boiled down to fear. It also boils down to the question, "Am I enough?" and those with the Butthole Syndrome will manipulate a "yes" to that answer by force.

But that doesn't work, does it? Just because others are afraid of you doesn't mean they respect you; it just means they're afraid of you. It also doesn't mean you feel good about yourself. The quality of your life is only a reflection of how you *feel* about it, remember. You may appear strong, powerful, in control and significant for a time, but you end up in a far worse place in the end.

Jackie Lewis illustrated this point poignantly. I met Jackie on vacation in the cliffs of Negril, Jamaica, when I visited her breathtaking wellness spa, *Jackie's on the Reef.* Unbeknownst to me, this 72-year-old beauty had a story of her own to contribute, having spent several years in the fast lane of the fashion industry as the owner of the first clothing store in Soho, New York. She tells how the Butthole Syndrome manifested for her:

"Have you seen the movie 'The Devil Wore Prada?' Basically, that was me; I was a bitch on wheels and didn't know it. I thought that's who I was supposed to be. When you're operating from this 'outer world,' you don't know that you are mean.

"You don't know you're offending people. You don't know you're hurting people. You just assume this is the way life is, and when you start reflecting, you realize how many people you've hurt, how many people you've stepped on. You're waking up. And when you wake up, it's sad."

Women, in particular, are falling victim to this more and more because of a belief that in order to run with the "big dogs," they've got to be like them. My friend Winter Baserva is a fantastic Realtor in the Atlanta market and has been featured on HGTV's hit TV show "House Hunters." She shares:

"I had taken on a very masculine version of myself because I had to; I had to adapt. But I have started becoming aware and now I realize that instead of putting my foot down, if I speak softly to somebody, I tend to have more power with them, both men and women. So my old school of thought was, okay, if they push, I push 10 times harder. If they say this, I'll say that 10 times louder. But my new thought is that feminine power really can work out."

Who are you in the workplace, in the classroom or on the basketball court? Are you known as the company "butthole" to the point that people are smiling in your face and flipping you off behind your back? More importantly, what really drives that attitude? Are you trying to prove you are enough and demand respect, or are you afraid of losing the respect you've earned? Yes, it feels good to look significant in the eyes of other people, but when you strip down to bra and boxers, how do you feel about the person looking back at you in the mirror?

Bringing the Noise

Ever met a person whose calendar is booked up weeks in advance? Every free moment is penciled in with meetings, happy hours, weekend brunches, activities, recreation, trips, board meetings, volunteer work, parties, movies, nightclubs, networking, galas, dates. . . *sheesh*. I'm winded just writing about it! The activities in (and of) themselves are fine, it's the motive that's in question. On the surface, it reads as though this person is really living life to the fullest. But are they?

Elliott is a vice president for a plastics company. He recalls:

"I was at a top consulting firm. I had a cell phone with CEOs numbers in it and, from a third-person's perspective, I was wildly successful. But I felt incapable because I had been thrown off my path by huge emotional relationship turmoil. To cope, I invested in a lot of activities, but there was no life or personal productivity. It was just a bunch of activities. I see a lot of people do that all the time—activity with no productivity. 'I go to this group. I do this and I have all these freaking activities.' Yeah, but did you really contribute anything today? That's the question."

If you fall into this category, realize that when you stop the noise, you then get to face the music. I say that you "get" to face the music instead of you "have" to face the music because the music is clarity, and clarity is such a gift.

If you want to truly have a return of fulfillment in your life, it is crucial to give yourself the space to figure out what you really want and how you can get it. That always requires facing your fears and sitting alone in the dark with them—minus the numbing noise.

Hiding Behind Achievement

Another key way fast-laners cope with low self-worth is by hiding behind their achievements. My friend Anton is a very successful serial entrepreneur in Denmark. He has started 14 businesses in 18 years. Like many fast-laners in the wrong direction, Anton prioritized his business at the expense of the other areas of his life: his health, his friendships and his intimate relationship. At some point, he realized something very profound about the motivation for his success:

> "For me, it was hard to go in and fix my relationship because that's not where I had the experience of succeeding," he said. "Just because I had been in a relationship for a number of years didn't mean I had a great relationship. So, I'd try to fill up my needs with the business.
>
> After a while, I became afraid of succeeding because after you've succeeded, after you've earned a million dollars or whatever the goal is, then it's like, 'What's next?' Deep down inside, you know what's next is that you should fix the other areas in your life. But you procrastinate by telling yourself, 'I have to finish this and that before I take care of my relationship, before I can be social, before I can fix my health, before I get spiritual.' And that got me a little scared of succeeding in business sometimes, because after the success, I'd have no more excuses not to deal with the rest of me. Now I see the motivation behind all those startups."

OMG! I totally related to everything Anton said. A few years ago, I was just embarking on a new business, and I told a girlfriend that I would be ready for a relationship in about three years—that's how long I thought it would take to get my business up and running consistently. She thought it was the most asinine thing she had ever heard; I thought she just didn't get it. I didn't realize it at the time, but I was looking for my business success to validate me as a great catch for a man. The odds of succeeding with a small business are slim, at best, and in my heart I didn't want a man to see me fumbling around trying to figure out the entrepreneurship thing.

The truth is, if you're consistently shooting for higher in your life, you are *always* fumbling around at some vulnerable stage of achievement, but I didn't quite see it that way. Fortunately, my friend was wise enough to call me out on my crap, and I eventually ended up in an amazing relationship while building the business. That relationship turned out to be a wonderful breath of fresh air, and I would have missed out had I not begun to see my value separate from my ambitions.

When we are in the grip of the Fraud Syndrome, we mask it in many ways, but the symptoms of self-worth deficiency are unmistakable. Here are some other common and fairly obvious coping signs:

Food is king—Just because you may pig out on more expensive food in the fast lane doesn't mean an addiction to it is any less indicative of self-esteem issues;

You're the consummate socialite—Your life is all about partying, clubbing and hitting all the right spots, and you find it hard to be still, be quiet or be alone;

Excessive status indicators—You have a checklist and need to hang in "this" circle, or be in the know with "this" group of people;

You pride yourself on the chase—If you're churning through women (or men) without true gratification, it's time to check yourself;

You use drugs and alcohol as an escape—You don't have to be a lush to use alcohol as an escape. If you find yourself plopped on the couch with a glass of wine or beer most nights, it's time to question;

You are bartering for love—Otherwise known as people pleasing, bartering for love is a little deceptive because your motives can appear to be so much about other people when, in actuality, they're all about you. You may find yourself giving to people or doing things to win friendship, love, acceptance and approval. With this motive, you will often feel disappointed, wondering why the very thing you want continues to elude you. You must value *yourself* before anyone else's validation will satisfy you.

If this chapter applied to you and you admitted some hard truths, I applaud you because that takes a ton of courage. By now, you should have received the memo that your coping mechanisms aren't enough. While they may mask the symptoms, they don't cure the ailment.

So how can you cope differently?

First, become a giver to the world and not a taker. When you are a taker, your focus is on how much money you can make, how much influence you can have and how much attention you can receive in a particular situation. As a result, you will always be on a competitive plane relative to other people, and you will constantly feel insecure because there is always someone making more money, always someone more influential and always someone garnering, or threatening to garner, more attention.

When you're a taker, you're never satisfied with what you get. I'm not saying money, influence, the desire for love, etc., are unimportant. But when you go into situations and *give* these things to others without the need for something in return to validate you, then you're free, and you will be amazed how much more money, influence, attention, love and opportunities will come your way, minus the manipulative schemes you maybe accustomed to.

It's easier said than done, for sure, and don't be surprised that you can't simply willpower the negative thoughts away. You may need to do some kind of personal growth, attend a transformational seminar, work with a life coach. . . or all of the above! I spent thousands of dollars working on *me,* spiritually, mentally and otherwise, because I had been conditioned for years to not value myself in the right ways. All I know from personal experience is that when you are a giver with the right motives, you will always find yourself advancing—in life, in business, on the job, socially, you name it.

Second, develop the belief system that you can always figure things out. Whatever the circumstance, when the time comes to deal with it, you will have all that it takes to figure it out. If you look back on your life right now, you will affirm this is true. Even in your most confusing, fearful times, when you stopped flailing about chaotically, you likely discovered that you were able to tread the waters of life. When Audrey decided to leave her human resources consulting career and launch a non-profit, she shared:

> **"I HAD A REASONABLE** degree of self-confidence that I could figure it out. That's one thing that I always believe to be true about myself, and hopefully other people think it's true about themselves as well. I might not know the answer. I might not have all the resources and the materials. I'm definitely not the smartest cookie in the room, but I trust myself enough to be able to figure it out."

What kept me in a sinking business partnership for so long was I didn't have the confidence that I could figure it out on my own. Yet all of my experiences prior to that partnership and afterward were evidence to the contrary. Now I have 100 percent belief that I can help *anyone* who comes in contact with me as a coach.

There is not a client I can't help or an audience I can't inspire. If there were someone better to serve that client than me, that client would be in front of... someone else. The fact they sought me for coaching, strategy or motivation is sufficient evidence that I'm their girl! So, if an opportunity is presented to me and it makes sense, I always say, "Yes!" first—then worry about how to do it later. Sometimes that "how" sounds like, "How in the H-E-double hockey sticks is that going to work out?" But it has never failed me.

Again, look back on your own life, and you might see this is true for you, too. Your mind will likely go straight to the times when things didn't work out as you hoped or when you *think* you didn't figure it out. You might have a very different perspective after reading the upcoming chapter on failure.

Finally, you'll grow more confident in your own self-worth when you quit judging other people! I have been in a few audiences where the question was posed, "How many of you are worried about what other people think of you right now?" Often, 99 percent of the hands shoot up. Isn't it funny that the very people you are concerned about impressing are preoccupied thinking about what *you* think of *them!*

Says Gabriela, a successful social media marketer:

"A personal fear for me is that people are going to make fun of me. If I really put my-

> ## Conversations in the Fast Lane
>
> ✓ Do you identify with any of the coping mechanisms outlined in the chapter?
>
> ✓ How easy is it for you to give in business, personal and social circumstances without the expectation of being given to in return?
>
> ✓ How confident are you to figure it out when it comes to uncertain circumstances, and how does that affect your willingness to take risks?
>
> ✓ How often do you find yourself being critical of other people, their value, accomplishments and ambitions? How does that correlate to your fear of being judged and criticized by other people?
>
> ✓ How does your level of self-worth affect how you cope with life's discomforts?

self out there and become vulnerable, people are just going to laugh."

The truth is, they will. Haven't you laughed at somebody for something? And no, you weren't laughing *with* them; you were laughing at them, and it was probably behind their back. Perhaps they were launching a product you thought was useless or acting in a movie you thought was garbage —and now that person is laughing themselves all the way to the bank!

So why should you be exempt?

Judgment happens. It's a basic fact of life. Within 15 seconds of meeting someone, you've judged whether you will like them and whether they will like you. Women are gifted with eyeing another woman passing on the street and within a millisecond conjuring an entire profile of a person they've never met! "She's a this. She's a that. She's probably also this other." If you're a woman reading this book, you know exactly what I'm talking about.

The reason we are so afraid of being judged, criticized and rejected is we realize we do that to other people. We know the depths of our judgment. We know the extent to which we can break down another person: their looks, personality, intellect, our perception of their talents, worth and value. We know the depths of our own jealousy and insecurities. We know how hurt someone could be by our judgment, and we're scared for someone to judge us in the same way.

It's not necessarily "bad" that we do this—assess and judge. In a way, it's a survival trait. If you consider all the thousands of pieces of information coming at you at any time during the day, you realize that categorizing and sorting this information is vital. It's a survival skill of sorts. Some things are critical to focus on, other things are not so important. It's the same with meeting people. That's why we assess or judge them immediately. The problem comes when we categorize people's intrinsic worth and gifts as being superior or inferior to our own.

I've learned there is a freedom that comes when I am unfazed by other people's opinions of me. I've also recognized that freedom comes at a price, and the price is that I am now super conscious of when I am critical of other people. It really is a boomerang effect. The more critical I am of other people and their value, the more concerned I am of what people think of me, and that's a catalyst for some fast lane, wrong direction coping mechanisms for sure.

Who are you?
You aren't what you do.
You are not your successes.
You are not your failures.
Who are you... *really?*

CHAPTER 5

••••

Identity Theft

EVER KNOWN SOMEONE trying to quit smoking but having a hard time? Maybe it was you at some point. Whether or not you have been a smoker, think about the behavior of a non-smoker. They refuse to smoke under any circumstances. Someone who is "trying to quit smoking" has to think about it because their decision to smoke is situational. They may be stressed, facing a deadline or need to relax, and any one of those situations might present a justifiable reason to inhale. Why? Because they're not a non-smoker—they're someone who is *trying to quit* smoking.

You see, the strongest force in the human nature is to be consistent with who you are or how you see yourself—your identity. *Random House Dictionary* defines identity as "the sense of self, providing sameness and continuity in personality over time and sometimes disturbed in mental illnesses, as in schizophrenia."

If you have been in the fast lane going in the wrong direction for any length of time, you no doubt relate to the feeling of being "disturbed in mental illness." In fact, I have wondered which of my personalities was running my life on a few occasions!

The point is, no matter how much willpower you exert to the contrary, you will eventually end up behaving in a way that is consistent with your identity, whether that's behaving like a non-smoker who never smokes or behaving like someone who is trying to quit smoking and does so under "justifiable" circumstances.

If I've lived my whole life as a screw-up, I will miraculously find every way to screw up my life—in my relationships, job and business. It's like a magnet, because that's who I *am*—a screw-up! And I will do whatever it takes, consciously or unconsciously, to be consistent with that identity.

If you see yourself as fat, you are going to do what fat people do. If you view yourself as unworthy in a relationship, you will do what unworthy people do. If you view yourself as a "super achiever," you will do what super achievers do… and there rests a really big problem for many, many people.

I call it "Identity Theft."

Who Do They Say I Am?

Phillip illustrates how the concept of "Identity Theft" showed up early in his adult life:

"When people asked what I wanted to be, I didn't know. But I was good at math and I was good at science, so I became (you guessed it) an engineer.

"As I got older, people asked why I chose Stanford University for college. Simply, I chose Stanford because I got in. At my boarding school, if you get into a college like Stanford, you go—no questions asked.

"In college, I had all the social accolades and everybody's respect, but I still felt like I knew I was searching for something even though I was at one of the top universities. All these expectations were built that didn't necessarily mirror my belief set, but I got so much reinforcement for them. When I was 18 or 19, going to Stanford from my hometown, everybody looked at me like a superstar. I didn't have to actually accomplish anything. That was the 'potential' stage of life; I was a success because I had 'potential.'

"I wanted to believe I was a success, but the things people viewed as demonstration of my success weren't things that were important to me. But I didn't know that because I hadn't taken the time to identify the things that were really important to me.

"Outwardly, people thought that I was pretty well put together. In reality, I was torn up emotionally at Stanford. I was doing well in classes, but a lot of people didn't know I would go back to my room and just sit there. I wasn't capable of doing anything else. I wasn't capable of studying, I wasn't capable of doing anything.

"Fortunately, I was gifted enough to pick up class work without doing an exceptional amount of studying. Though I don't think I had a critical mental illness, it's quite possible I was clinically depressed. All I know is I wasn't in a good place mentally.

"Few people know it, and I didn't tell my mom, but I dropped out of school for a quarter of my senior year. I withdrew my registration and literally just didn't go to school. Instead, I spent the entire quarter reading the Bible and working. Most people had no clue because I was still at school hanging out, but I wasn't really in school. That decision forced me to extend graduation by another year, but it was probably one of the most defining moments in my life.

"The No. 1 thing I learned during that time was that I don't have to do anything. I used to live this life where I felt I had to do so much. I had to do X, Y and Z, and that was driving me. I realized after that timeout that I don't have to do anything. I don't have to get up in the morning. I don't have to go to class. I don't have to do anything. Don't get me wrong; I have to live with the repercussions of what I do and don't do, but for the first time I realized I had a choice. As basic of a concept as that is, I had a *choice*. began to understand why I was doing what I was doing beyond the usual reason of 'this is what you're supposed to do to be successful in life.' "

What happened with Phillip is common for many fast-laners. Who we are is a function of who other people say we are and what other people say we should do to be successful. We unwittingly embrace that script as our personal identity without questioning whether we should own that identity. The desires other people have for us, or that we have for ourselves, are not necessarily bad; they're usually coming from positive intent. There is nothing wrong with being at the top of the leader board in sports, ministry, business or politics—unless you *don't want to be* at the top of that particular leader board.

The sad reality is most people don't have the early epiphany Phillip did, nor do they have the courage at his age, or any age, to stop and regroup.

When we are young, it is almost easier to take a timeout because, as Phillip noted, that is the stage of "potential." There's expectation, but you don't have to deliver on that expectation just yet. As you mature, professionally and otherwise, there is so much more intangible value placed on your chosen identity—real or perceived—that the weight of change is far heavier.

As you continue to allow your identity to be shaped by external views of success and happiness, a funny thing happens: those external views eventually become your own. Sounds a bit like that "disturbed in mental illness" concept we mentioned earlier, right? Here's what my friend Hillary, a chief of staff, had to say:

" **WHEN I WAS** young, I was invisible except that I was smart, so as I got older, I wanted to be unique in some way. I went from being one of 60 at my first company, to one of 30 at my second, to being the one person with all the information in my current role. That's my identity. I need to feel indispensable. I can't be ordinary. "

In the grown-up stage, no one is forcing you to believe what it means to be successful, and there is some part of you that realizes you don't know where those beliefs really came from and if they are authentically yours. You don't know whose identity you have taken on, but it seems to have happened in a blink. All you know is that you're not happy with who you are and every decision you now make reinforces an identity that you are wholly unfulfilled by.

No offense if you're an attorney, but I don't meet a lot of lawyers who like the practice of law… but Karen actually does, and she's quite good. She illustrated the tricky nature of "Identity Theft" when she shared:

"Because I didn't value my skill as much as I valued a superstar writer's, I would move away from what I liked to do to what my image of success was. The example I looked up

> **Conversations in the Fast Lane**
>
> ✓ When was the last time you stopped to really question what you want, and why?
>
> ✓ When you think about who you are and what you want, how much of that is a function of other people's blueprints and opinions?
>
> ✓ Is there any area of your life where you are chasing an identity that's not your own, whether in your career or in relationship or in some other area?
>
> ✓ What actions are you taking in your life because you feel like you should instead of because you want to do it?
>
> ✓ Again, who are you?

······································

to was the appellate lawyer, but the appellate lawyer's strengths were not my strengths. I'm not a writer; instead, I like talking to people. The former image was what I thought was the 'super lawyer.' Each one of my career moves was angling me to more of that 'super lawyer' image, so I didn't look for jobs that would enhance the skills I already had."

Ding! Ding! Ding! I hope you're catching her point loud and clear. When you stop to evaluate what you want at your core—in relationship, career or lifestyle design—that desire is usually pretty clear. Identity Theft comes into play because we get tripped up on *how* it should present itself in our lives. Karen really liked law, but for years she was playing somebody else's part in the law field, taking on roles that made her unhappy and failing to play to her natural strengths.

The idea of "Identity Theft" goes beyond career. It was the reason Alisha got married:

> "ALL MY FRIENDS had gotten married in their early 20s, and they were now on baby one or baby two. I was still single, and I was working like crazy. Marriage was a bad decision all the way around, and it was a decision that I made because there was this thing inside of me that felt like my package was incomplete. I thought, 'I've got a good job, but I don't have the husband, I don't have the kids, I don't have the house. I guess I better get that part wrapped up now.'
>
> So I met a man 20 years older and we got married. Two years later, we divorced. We were terrible and horrible to each other. At 26, everything blew up and there were pieces everywhere. That was really the first time in my life that I sat back and started questioning what I really believed versus what I thought I believed because that's what everyone told me I should believe."

Again, nothing wrong with wanting to be married, but who told Alisha it had to happen almost fresh out of college? Being a talented lawyer is fine, but why did Karen feel she had to be an appellate lawyer to qualify as a talented attorney? Being preeminent in your field is fine, but why do you have to be in a field you loathe?

I inadvertently delayed my call as a speaker, coach and motivator for a while because I thought I first had to earn my success doing real estate investing, network marketing and a host of other endeavors that I *hated*. Identity Theft told me I just had to be successful at something—*anything*—because that success is what would qualify me to inspire and serve people.

I failed to realize my greatest success would come pursuing the avenues I was most gifted and satisfied by, not the pursuits I had to work overtime in just to be competent. I wanted to achieve before I fell in love because I failed to realize the truest kind of love would come from a man who would believe in me even at the small beginnings of my business, not just when the tough times were over. I had gotten it so twisted, and that twist affected how I made decisions for years.

When I finally dug deep into myself, I realized that the core of what I wanted—the success, massive impact, influence and contribution to the world—remained unchanged. But who I chose to become to achieve those things changed drastically. I was no longer chasing whims of success that offered fortune with no fulfillment, nor did I have to align my timetable or life design to anyone else's. I knew who I was.

Who are you?

"I feel the need for speed."
— Tom Cruise as "Maverick" in *Top Gun*

CHAPTER 6

The Need For Speed

WHEN I DECIDED to write *Fast Lane, Wrong Direction,* one of the first people I interviewed said there is a difference between writing the book and living the book. That's really profound. He suggested I go through the process and "feel" the book live as opposed to just writing to get it done. He was so right, but I admit my first thought was, "Now, that's a real slow lane way to look at it."

The truth is, I have lived every topic of this book as I've written it—from wondering if the content is truly valuable to changing my completion deadline so many times I lost count. But this topic, the need for speed, is the one I was most challenged by through the writing process, and it's also an area on which I can reflect proudly and acknowledge so much growth and surrender over the years. The need for speed is a big contributor to a lot of wasted time, money and overall unhappiness for people.

> "We've grown up in a society where everything needs to happen right now. I need to start my business on Tuesday. I need to have a product out by Thursday, and I need to make sure that product is selling a million units by next Saturday! I felt like a failure because my product came out late. But the truth is, there is always someone who is going to need what I do."
> — *Abigail, entrepreneur*

One of the awesome qualities about fast-laners is we get stuff done—fast! On the other hand, the Achilles' heel of fast-laners is we get stuff done fast — complete with Band-Aids, duct tape, twisty ties and pantyhose to hold it all together. We will break our necks to meet some imaginary window for success, largely based on some record a guru or mentor set as an example. It goes something like this:

"If so and so started their business and hit their first million in two years, then that's what I'm going to do! I don't need to eat, sleep or shower (okay, maybe shower). The friends can wait, I don't have time to date, momma knows I love her, but I'm on a mission… to get the product done, to make partner, to win the gold medal. And I need to do it now-now-now-now-now! I'm late. I'm behind. I need to catch up. Let's go!"

When marketing their expertise, gurus often fail to mention it took them eight years of trial and error and investment to learn the skills that equipped them to make that first million in two years. They fail to share they would give all their money to get back what they sacrificed in exchange for speed.

Minor marketing oversight… *Right*.

In the meantime, we are wearing ourselves out, we're unhappy, we can't celebrate, and when we finally get "there" (wherever there is!), it's not nearly as satisfying as we thought it would be. Worse, we can't remember any of the joys of the journey along the way.

Your need for speed has various roots. You might be broke and eager to no longer be broke, so the faster you make money, the faster you are no longer broke. I've been there. For others, it's rooted in ego; you want to be the youngest X or the fastest Y. Still, for others, it's rooted in this internal sense of failure. If you don't accomplish something in the same time frame as someone else, then somehow you're not as good as they are. Whatever the reason, the need for speed at the expense of mastery, depth and quality or for the satisfaction of ego never has lasting power and *always* creates a tremendous amount of insecurity and discontentment.

We can all agree that every great success story starts with a small beginning. Apple started in a garage. Facebook started in a dorm room. Walmart started as a five and dime.

Fast-laners, however, rarely start anything small.

It's great to have big vision. The challenge is there is absolutely no shortcut for experience, and mastery of anything is a function of time and experience. Many fast-laners disrespect the value of time and experience, so they show contempt for the small beginnings. There's no time to lay a strong foundation for the business or develop solid processes because you've set your sights on your first federal government contract. There's no time to build a solid relationship because you're scanning your checklist to see if they are "The One." Whatever literary accomplishment you've made in the moment is never good enough because what you really need is a *New York Times* bestselling book to say you're somebody.

What you don't realize in the quest for speed is that you will be ill-equipped to handle the volume that big fat government deal will generate because your systems are shoddy. My friend Bianca is a foreclosure expert and learned this lesson in true fast-lane fashion (you know how we do it!). She sponsored a nationwide sweepstakes for homeowners and a full year of mortgage payments was covered for the winner. So much good came out of this effort because it was a tremendous windfall for the lucky winner and a huge business lesson for Bianca. She recounts:

> **WHEN I DID** the sweepstakes, my energy was crap, my money was crap, my focus was crap, but I wanted to do this thing. It was funny because somebody told me not to do the sweepstakes, and I thought, 'What are you talking about? Of course I'm going to do the sweepstakes! Of course! It will be great!'
>
> If I hadn't done it, I might be in a very different place in my life right now, but I'm glad I did because it showed how little foundation there was under what I was doing. You are the foundation of your business. If you are not happy, healthy, strong and focused, then you may be able to pull things off for a little while, but you can't sustain yourself for the long run.
>
> The same goes for your business. If you don't have the foundation of a strong plan and a good idea that has taken time to develop, that you know every part of and can talk about it in your sleep… If you don't have a good financial base for it and the foundation of all the small things that take a long time to pull together, then you're totally building on sand. Everybody wants the flash, but if there is no foundation to your flash, the flash goes away and then—*BOOM!*—you're left with nothing.

How many of us have dived headlong into an idea, business, career path or relationship because we had to get there now-now-now-now-now? And in the process we take risks, but not just any risks. We take stupid risks, cheap risks and not-well-thought-out risks.

One of my mentors says, "GSTF: Get Stuff Done Fast." As a recovering perfectionist, I appreciate that commitment to just "get 'er done," and I will pay good money to coaches, trainers and experts to show me how to shave years off my learning curve. I call it "buying speed." I'm all about making quantum leaps in life with smart strategies in health, love, money and any other area that's important, and I highly suggest you make the investments in yourself to do the same.

What you cannot shorten, however, is experience. Contrary to what many believe, experience is not always a function of time or age; it is a function of, well, *experience*… the actual doing of *the thing*. Regardless of your title or income, when you know in your gut that you are not seasoned in your craft, you will feel insecure about your value in the marketplace, even when great opportunities come your way. When you know in your gut that you are not seasoned in a relationship, you may question whether you're with the right person, even as you're zooming along to the tune of wedding bells.

> ## **Conversations in the Fast Lane**
>
> ✓ In what ways does the "need for speed" show up in your life, both positively and negatively?
>
> ✓ Have you taken shortcuts in career, business or love? What were the results?
>
> ✓ When you are tempted to choose speed over quality, mastery or thoroughness, what fear usually drives you?
>
> ✓ What imaginary windows do you have in your life?
>
> ✓ How does having an imaginary window of success affect the progress you make in various areas of your life?

- - -

By "seasoned," I don't mean certifications and degrees, necessarily, though that could be a part of the measure for you. Bianca went back for her MBA as a result of her sweepstakes experience. I'm talking about taking the necessary steps to work right—not harder, not smarter, but *right*. When you do that, you avoid the meteoric ascent to stardom followed by the fizzle that comes when you've burn out of fuel.

Speed is good, just not at the expense of doing things right. Speed is good, just not at the expense of quality. Speed is good, just not when you're speeding out of fear of some loss. Check yourself and truly evaluate the quality of your outcomes, and make the conscious decision to slow down if you find those outcomes flawed.

> **"There were times when I tried to take shortcuts, and I basically had to learn the lesson all over again. Shortcuts take longer, in a nutshell."**
> — *Emerson, state politician*

Decide that you're in it for mastery. Mastery is not fly-by-night. If you take the time to read the biographies of venerable superstars and others you admire, their timelines will show that it took a heck of a long time for them to become an "overnight success." And those who opt for the shortcut rarely (if ever) have staying power.

Your mind may assault you with thoughts like, "I'll miss out. Somebody will take my spot. They'll beat me to the punch!"

That couldn't be farther from the truth; there's always enough—for you and everybody else. If you subscribe to that scarcity mindset, you'll always be afraid of missing out, and there will always be another spot for somebody else to take. Why? Because you're always advancing, so there's always another imaginary window. It never ends.

You can have quick monetary success; it happens all the time. But that doesn't mean you are successful in the living of your life. And truly, that's all that matters. What people don't realize is they will always be brought down to the level of their personal and spiritual growth. You will make the money, and somehow lose it. You will be elevated, then demoted. You can't fake mastery, integrity and authenticity—not for long.

Slow down so you can speed up.

There's no need to ever compare
yourself to someone else.
The world is waiting for you to do "you."
Nobody, I mean nobody, does that better than you.

CHAPTER 7
····
Nobody Does You Better Than You

HAVE YOU EVER found yourself fired up about the latest happenings in your life? Maybe you lost 10 pounds, or you bought a new car, or you released the first edition of your book.

Whatever it was, life was looking up!

That is… until you ran into your "Biggest Loser" friend who shed 25 pounds to your 10, or the dude who got the newer, better, faster car for cheaper than you paid, or the colleague who was on TV talking about their book while you were peddling your masterpiece to a couple hundred Facebook friends. There is no faster way to douse cold water on our accomplishments than comparing where we are to where someone else is, and I can't think of any flaw more pervasive in the fast lane make-up than the obsession with comparisons.

Let's be real: Competition is an essential part of life. There can only be one Super Bowl-winning team a year, one president of the United States, one Miss America pageant queen. But when it comes to the game of life, as "preschoolish" as it may sound, everybody can be a winner. The rules to the game of life are different and, consequently, the rules for experiencing fast lane, *right direction* are hinged on our ability to free ourselves from the negative impact of comparing our progress with that of other people.

I'm embarrassed to admit this, but I was watching an episode of "American Idol" one night, and something got me to thinking about Ryan Seacrest and how rich he must be, given the reality show, radio show and all the other things he is doing. Then I thought, "I wonder how old he is." Everything in me hoped he was in his mid 40s, because somehow that would make me feel better about myself, as if I still had time to reach the level of my own ambitions. So, of course, I went to the all-knowing source of information (Google) and discovered, to my dismay, that he was only a few months older than me.

Are you freakin' kidding me?!?!

Then I began to compare our timelines… When did he start broadcasting? When did he land his first commercial gig? When did this start, when did that start? It turns out Seacrest practically had a microphone in his hand before he could walk, and throughout his entire life he took steps that moved him in the direction of his passion.

My dismay had nothing to do with his riches; I envied his ability to F.O.C.U.S (Follow One Course Until Successful). When we look at his professional life, at least, we see the fruit of that focus and the years of seasoning and experience that have culminated into his current success. Why couldn't it have happened that way for me? Why did I have to flail about for over a decade trying to discover my purpose? Why was my life marked by a dead-end pursuit of unfulfilling ambitions?

I would have "focused" and paid my dues if only I had a *focus*. Why not me? I could feel the engine of comparison revving up, and I knew that would only put me in the "my life sucks" state, which is always unproductive, right? Instead, I chose to get inspired by the possibilities of what a focused life could produce and recognize that we each have a purpose for our lives, and that purpose is fulfilled through great highs and great lows; no one escapes either end of the spectrum.

All we see with Ryan Seacrest is the flash; we don't know the darkness, and that's the lie of omission that comparison creates. We don't know what people went through to get what they got, how they might suffer to keep it or who they are behind closed doors. So often, when we are "boo-hooing" about why we aren't where someone else is, we have failed to read to the end of our own story.

I can't imagine doing anything else with my life than what I am currently doing, and I know that purpose was revealed through the pain, frustration and confusion of the prior years. When I coach my clients, I can literally articulate their pain in ways that blow them away. I can anticipate their next moves, what they're thinking, what their insecurities are without them saying a word. I can ask that profound question that will cut right to the heart of everything they're trying to avoid. Why? Because I have been there. And in the same way that I couldn't possibly do what Ryan Seacrest does in the way that he does it, nobody can do me better than me.

Joey is a professional speaker and owner of a branding firm in Denver. What's awesome about Joey is his ability to "switch" lanes in his life. When he notices something isn't working, he is quick to course-correct and explore a new route. You'll learn more about Joey later in the book and how his philosophy propelled him from being a criminal defense attorney in Iowa to a very successful entrepreneur. But for now, let's focus on how comparisons affected him in the earlier stages of his business:

"I was bumping into law school buddies out and about in Washington D.C., and, of course they're all saying, 'I'm on the partner track at whatever law firm,' and here I was starting my own business—no health insurance, working out of my apartment, eating peanut butter and jelly sandwiches, doing everything to fund the business. It didn't take me too long to recognize I was happier than they were. When that really started to sink in, it helped me justify what I was doing. It was a few years afterward when I became fully comfortable with the fact that I had walked away from the lucrative power attorney career to start my own business and really do what I like to think of as lifestyle design—creating and shaping the kind of life I wanted instead of the kind of life others expected."

Who hasn't had one of those situations where you wish you could crawl into a hole at the sight of somebody you envy? Often it's not the "I wish he were dead" kind of envy, but more of the "I suck" kind of envy. That envy goes back to the very two questions we revealed earlier in the book:

1.) Am I enough?

2.) Will I be loved?

When Joey and I discussed how those questions applied to his feeling of inadequacy, he said:

> "YOU HIT THE nail on the head. It's 'where I was' compared to where others were. Those were the two questions that were screaming through my head at that time and, quite frankly, still come up on a regular basis. I'm just shy of 38, and a lot of friends I went to law school with are now full partners in major law firms, which means they're pulling in $500,000 to a million dollars a year. My business, while very successful, is not pulling in a $1 million salary for me.
>
> What I realized I had that I don't think my colleagues had was that I travel a ton, and I come and go as I please," he continued. "If I were to decide tomorrow to stay home and read a book, I could. And that freedom is really empowering to me. I sacrifice a lot for my company, but it's my company, not someone else's. And I like to think I keep a pretty decent balance on what's worth sacrificing and what's not."

This is not about bashing attorneys or Corporate America; there are plenty of people who thrive in these roles and are highly fulfilled by them. This is about clarity for what you want in your life, independent of what somebody else has. Joey wanted the freedom that came with successful entrepreneurship. Every entrepreneur will tell you that freedom comes with lots of sacrifices and some dark times. Yet even after the sacrifices and dark times, if you are still comparing your business success to someone else's, you will never have the freedom you crave.

> ## Conversations in the Fast Lane
>
> ✓ In the last week, to whom have you compared yourself? How did it make you feel, and what actions resulted from it?
>
> ✓ Have you ever thought to ask a person how they achieved what you envy? Why or why not?
>
> ✓ What do you actually gain by comparing yourself to others, whether to people you view as below you or above you?
>
> ✓ Who would you be if you deliberately rid yourself of competition in the game of life? What would change?
>
> ✓ Who has something you want, and what could you learn from them if you had the guts, courage, heart, strength or balls to ask?

You will never enjoy whatever success you currently have, whether that's making your first million dollars or having your first month where revenues exceed expenses. Moreover, you will find yourself chasing a moving target, because there is always someone with more money, a hotter wife or a better body. You might one-up the next person here or there, but the comparison game is one you ultimately cannot win.

None of us will ever stop comparing ourselves to other people; it is human nature. But when we know what we really want, we're better able to separate our personal journey from the next person's and use those comparisons to learn from the next person rather than competing with them. Wallace Wattles wrote in the *Science of Getting Rich* that "you do not have to covet the property of others, or look at it with wishful eyes; no man has anything of which you cannot have the like, and that without taking what he has from him."

When you deliberately rid yourself of competition in the game of life and recognize that your success, happiness and worth are never relative to someone else's, you will succeed… and you will enjoy it. In fact, when you encounter someone who has what you want, you will have the humility to learn from them, to seek advice from them and thereby obtain any and everything you want. You will be able to ask, "How did you lose the weight and keep it off? How do you maintain a harmonious marriage? What did you do to get promoted so quickly?"

Removing that competition is one of the hardest qualities to master because it takes guts, courage, heart, strength, balls and any other synonym you can think of to finally achieve. But that's what I call true "Braveheart" valor, and those who exercise it become world class more effortlessly, and their personal satisfaction is no longer at the whim of the next man's ego trip.

You can't achieve perfection,
but you can achieve some pretty
ugly manifestations of it.

CHAPTER 8
••••
The Autobiography Of a Failure

THERE ARE SEVEN words that represent the core message of this chapter: Make room in your life for failure.

Some fast-laners don't know what it's like to have a tail-spinning, gut-wrenching, lift-your-face-out-of-the-mud kind of failure. Sure, you've had some disappointments, but you've worked hard and somehow things have always worked out—in school, work, extracurricular activities. You have earned your success rightfully, yet there's an intense fear of being out of control and not having a calculated "win."

For others, you have tasted that kind of failure and vowed to never, ever go back there again. Either way, when failure happens, or the *illusion* of failure happens, it feels as if you have been sucker punched. You don't know what to do or how to react. Worse, you're more likely to propel yourself into what you know will be the wrong direction to avoid the pain of that failure.

> "When I quit my job I thought everything was going to work out; things had always been really easy for me. But the fact of the matter is that for three and a half years now I've been working to build a business that has been completely unprofitable. If you had told me when I left that job I wouldn't make enough money to live at the level I was living before and yet still I would find a way to make things happen, I never would have believed you… and I probably wouldn't have quit my job."
>
> — *Dolores, entrepreneur*

Like Dolores, I didn't make room in my life for failure when I started my business, so when failure hit (and it hit with a vengeance), I saw it as an indictment on my worth. The fear of experiencing more failure colored everything I did. It took me years before I could enjoy the freedom of being self-employed because I was so afraid of failing. Wallace Wattles says in the *Science of Getting Rich* that "when you make a failure, it is because you have not asked for enough. Keep on, and a larger thing than you were seeking will certainly come to you." That has proven true for me in business, career and relationships, among other things.

Failure is something many people desperately avoid, yet fast-laners have developed some destructive habits that actually contribute to the very failure we dread. These *developed* habits are not inherent. We have been conditioned to behave in certain ways that actually block us from strategically designing a life that will juice us to the max.

If we were to review the DVD of the failures in our lives, I have no doubt they would be marked by one, if not all three, of the precursors below. If one or more of these habits is prevalent in your personality, failure is on the horizon, and it's likely a failure of the "ugly kind."

Failures of the ugly kind are ones you look back on and know you could have avoided. Most people recognize they have these habits, but they don't change course because these habits preserve the very core of their self-worth and identity. As mentioned in prior chapters, we'll do anything to preserve our identity, and all our fears boil down to two root questions: "Will I be loved?" and "Am I enough?" The fear of failure is no exception.

There's one caveat. Though no one *likes* failure, by necessity, entrepreneurs develop a tolerance for failure and even an expectation it will happen. You only need to look at the statistics for small business viability to know the odds are stacked against your success. But a tolerance for failure is no excuse for self-inflicting it unnecessarily.

Failure Habit No. 1: The DIY (Do-It-Yourself) Syndrome

"We handicap ourselves because we want to do everything by ourselves, to be this self-made millionaire. Nobody does anything by themselves. We don't reach out to the people that we meet, and when we do meet them, we have these fake conversations around what we've done."

– *Carla, entrepreneur*

If what Carla says describes you to a T, then you have a full-blown case of the DIY Syndrome, and phrases such as "I can figure this out," "I can make it happen," "I don't need to ask for help" run rampant through your head. DIY is tricky because you can likely pinpoint a few areas in your life where you are receiving help. You may have a mentor advising you on the next steps of your career or a joint-venture partner who brings a competency that you lack to the project. That alone should be all the evidence you need to skip this section altogether, right? You can pat yourself on the back and scratch this tip right off the list. One less piece of self-help mumbo jumbo to process....

Not so fast.

Before you mentally check out on this topic, take a closer look at the areas where you are struggling. I'm talking about those rarely disclosed parts of your life, career or business. It's those places where you think you *should* be able to figure it out, you *should* be able to make it happen on your own and you *should* have it all together that are wreaking havoc on the rest of your world. As the common adage goes, you're "shoulding all over yourself."

Seriously, if you manage 10 people at the office, how hard can it be to get along with your spouse at home? You don't need help for that. If you can coach a bunch of kids to be all they can be on the Little League field, certainly you can overcome your own mental hurdles and dream bigger for yourself. You should have these goals on lock, right? But in reality you're working harder than you need to, wasting more resources than you have to and probably not seeing the results you desire.

The DIY Syndrome is so insidious for fast-laners that I dedicate an entire chapter later in the book on how to overcome it and ask for the help you need. Whether it's with your health, your kids or your joy level, if there's some area where you're failing miserably, it's likely because you think you *should* be able to handle that area on your own.

Failure Habit No. 2: Perfection

You had to know this topic would come up, right? If there is a character trait more conducive to failing, it is the idea you have to be perfect. Beyond a commitment to quality, the desire for perfection will paralyze you to the extent you never go after the real desire of your heart for fear you can't do it right.

The time would have long passed for you to make an important decision or finish a big project or submit your contest entry because you spent so much time making things just a little bit better instead of learning the art of "good enough." I was a classic example. Some of us have this deep, dark place inside that feels we have to be perfect, even when logically we know that's completely untrue. We know it's impossible to be perfect, but we strive for perfection anyway.

I'm not going to make the argument that perfection is impossible—I have no doubt you know better. And if you are struggling with perfectionism, knowing that it's impossible does not keep you from acting in ways that totally subvert your success and fulfillment. What I will do is expose perfectionism for what it really is and illustrate why it will never get you what you want.

In truth, perfection is not about being better, it's about being enough. If you are without flaws, you can't be criticized, judged or rejected, right? Wrong. I say it yet again, all roads lead back to our two big questions from chapter 3: "Will I be loved?" and "Am I enough?" The irony is that in the pursuit of perfection, you lose the very thing you want, which is acceptance.

Think about it: How do you feel about people you believe have it all together? How do you treat people who come across as perfect? You may find that you envy them, at best, or can't stand them, at worst, even if the only reason for your disdain is they stir up your insecurities. Either way, you generally don't relate to them and you're reluctant to be around them. Why?

Because they're perfect, and we fear perfection as much as we admire it.

At some point, you may have been on the receiving end of this treatment with people judging you, withholding friendship or distancing themselves from you, because you're a person they perceive as having it all together. As humans, we admire excellence, but we relate to flaws. We gravitate to other people's weaknesses because it helps us to accept our own flaws and weaknesses with more grace. An equally important reason we gravitate to people's weaknesses is it helps us to trust them, to relate to them, opening a space for mutual vulnerability.

I didn't understand this point until I was in my 30s. Over the years, it would hurt my feelings when women, in particular, would not like me even though they didn't really know me. This was definitely present in high school, and as an adult, I noticed I just wasn't very close to other women.

The light bulb flickered on during a class on how to do TV interviews. I was being coached by Janine Driver, *New York Times* bestselling author of the book, *You Say More Than You Think*. We were doing mock situational interviews, and, of course, I wanted to do my part "perfectly." So, when it came time for feedback, Janine said, "I think you're coming across as stuck-up. You appear to be perfect, like you don't have a problem in the world. People in middle America, watching TV, want to hear from a real person with real problems and real solutions."

Wow. And that's when it came together for me.

I wanted to be perfect on TV so I would be good enough, so I would qualify as an expert, so I could give something of value to the people I served, but that "perfection" is the very thing that separated me from people. Janine's observation revolutionized my TV appearances from that point, and it revolutionized how I connect one-on-one with people. I am so much more open about my challenges, weaknesses, fears and screw-ups because that's what endears me to people. The skill of being able to admit perfection has opened more opportunities than just about any other skill set I have learned. Beyond business, however, it just makes for more authentic, enriching relationships.

If you want to be perfect for the sake of perfection, you can certainly do that, but you will find yourself alone and disconnected emotionally from other people—epic fail. If your pursuit of perfection is because somewhere deep inside you desire to be good enough, you must realize that you are good enough, not because of perfection, but in spite of imperfection. Do whatever you need to do—counseling, coaching, transformational work, prayer—to help you embrace that truth.

Failure Habit No. 3: Hiding from Criticism

The third precursor to the inevitable failure most of us experience comes down to our fear of criticism. My friend Carla in Failure Habit No. 1 gave one of the best descriptions of criticism. She said, "I hate criticism. To me, it's like somebody saying your baby is ugly."

Really, does it get any more truthful than that?

For most of us, criticism is to our ego like kryptonite is to Superman. We will avoid it at all costs and in doing so miss ever-important feedback that can accelerate our success, reveal our blind spots and protect us from land mines in our career, business, marriage, parenting—you name it. Granted, not all criticism is constructive, but in the big scheme of things, does that really matter?

If you took stock of the ratio of constructive, money-saving, life-giving feedback you receive from people versus the hurtful, ill-intentioned feedback, it's probably 50-to-1 in favor of the positive. Janine's feedback on how I came across on TV was so valuable because she uncovered my blind spot. Sure, it was uncomfortable to receive in front of the other students because her perception could not have been further from the truth of who I am at my core, but applying the constructive criticism instantly made me better. Had I refused to put myself in the position to be coached, who knows how long it would have taken me to progress?

You must learn to embrace criticism. No way around it. You will fail otherwise, and even when you experience bursts of success, you will be so tied in knots emotionally that you will not feel the joy of your victory. It's essential to reframe the concept of criticism and begin to see it as feedback. The word "criticism" carries a negative connotation— criticalness—and many people have linked criticism to a personal indictment of their worth. But if you open yourself to "feedback," you are opening to responses that bring about even better outcomes in your life.

That reframe is a marginal improvement, sure, but it won't have lasting value unless you know your worth as we talked about in chapter 3. When I am secure in my value, apart from anything I do or accomplish and apart from anybody else's validation, then I can proactively seek out feedback. My product pitch doesn't have to be perfect, the project can be incomplete, my shoes can be on the wrong feet, metaphorically speaking, and I can still soak up the golden nuggets of other people's insights.

One of my mentors, Dani Johnson, says this repeatedly and each time it rings true:

> **Conversations in the Fast Lane**
>
> ✓ Have you made room for failure in your life?
>
> ✓ Do you believe you must accomplish your goals on your own or do you openly accept input in your work, marriage, parenting and other facets of life?
>
> ✓ Do you struggle with perfectionism? If so, why? Are you trying to be better than someone else, or are you trying to be "enough?"
>
> ✓ Do you hide from criticism or do you proactively seek feedback?
>
> ✓ When you weigh your ego with your goals, which tends to weigh more, and how does that affect the action you choose to take or avoid?

"Weigh your ego with your goal and see which one weighs more."

I have shown that doing it yourself, pursuing perfection and/or hiding from criticism is cancerous to your overall fulfillment. The only reason we hang on to these habits is to protect our ego. In those moments of wrestling, weigh your ego with your goal and determine which one you're valuing more in that moment. If you value achieving the goal more, then you will humble yourself and do what it takes to achieve the goal, whether that's asking for help or soliciting feedback. When you know that's the right thing to do but are reluctant to do so, your ego weighs more in that moment.

You can camp out with your ego if you want, but your goal will suffer. You simply have to determine if preserving your ego is worth it to you.

Challenges are an inevitable part of life.
It's the suffering that's optional.

CHAPTER 9
••••
How to Get a 'High Return on Failure'

WHAT YOU LEARNED from the last chapter is there are three conditioned habits that lead most fast-laners to "failures of the ugly kind. "When you are in the throes of failure, whether it is of your own doing or you are a victim of circumstance, there is a way to get a "high return on failure," much like a high return on investment in business. These strategies are simple, but they are not easy. Mastering them, however, will equip you to breeze through the rough patches of life common to all of us.

Return on Failure Tip No. 1: Reframe Your Failure

Can you look back at a time in your life where something didn't go according to your plan, only to find out later it was the greatest gift that could have happened to you? It could have been a failed marriage, a plummeting business, a position you really wanted that went to someone else. We can all pinpoint something. In the moment, it's a real bummer, but in retrospect we thank God for that unanswered prayer.

An amazing quality about fast-laners is our dedication to whatever cause we pursue, but the drawback to our dedication is we often don't know when to walk away from a situation that no longer serves us. It is at these points we are poised for a letdown, as my friend Heinrich from Denmark describes:

"People are never willing to compromise their own identity. If you are caught up by it, it's very hard to make needed changes. That's why sometimes people are lucky if they get fired or their business goes wrong, or the relationship fails, or whatever. That's why they say everything happens for a purpose. I actually think people get so caught up by what they think they need that they don't know what their real needs are. Subconsciously, they may really want to get out of a situation, and sometimes the failure is the absolute best thing that could happen because the failure actually provides a way out."

The point Heinrich is making here is that sometimes failure happens because you are off-purpose. For many of us, we know we want out, we know a particular situation is not serving us, but for whatever reason we are unwilling to walk away. Singer-songwriter Gladys Knight penned a song that says, "Neither one of us wants to be the first to say good-bye," and if you find yourself in that situation with a job or a relationship, you will likely be *forced* to say good-bye, and that farewell may be in the form of failure.

My client Deborah says:

"**SOMETIMES YOU NEED** a pink slip in life to force you to go for it. Some of us get pushed off the ledge, some of us jump."

I hated everything about my years of real estate investing—the toilets, tenants, trash, government agents, auctions, investors, contractors, the whole nine. But in my mind, those efforts were going to lead me to financial freedom.

I was doing a four-property deal with a partner and we were going to renovate the properties and flip them. The seller on the transaction was an unsavory character, to say the least, which made the experience even less appealing. My partner and I had been renovating one of the four properties for a couple of months, had found another buyer to flip the property to, and were about two weeks away from making a nice chunk of change on the deal. We arrived at the property to do work one day only to find our key didn't work. The lock had been changed… by the new owner of the property!

The seller had sold the property at auction right after he signed the contract with me, *several months before*. Effectively, my partner and I were now trespassing on the property we had been pouring money into to renovate, not to mention the expenses of the other three properties. To sue the seller would have been an absolute waste of time and money because it turned out he had debtors all across the Eastern Seaboard, including family and delinquent child support. We'd have to just get in line. I was done.

I wasn't just done with the seller. I was done with that city. I was done with investing. *I was done.* I remember hitting I-95 south from Baltimore, and I never went back. I cut my losses and got completely out of the real estate game. It wasn't that the setback was insurmountable, but as Heinrich said, the failure provided me a way out of an already miserable situation. Had it not been for that sour experience and other wacky turns of events, I would have continued doing something that made me utterly miserable.

Why? Because real estate was my ticket to financial freedom, or so I thought. I would have stuck with it through all emotional, mental and physical costs. Getting jacked by a surly seller wasn't fun, but it literally turned out to be my "Get Out of Jail Free" card; I just didn't know it at the time.

One of my coaching members posed a question when she was considering whether she should have stayed on the partner track at her law firm. She asked, "If you succeed at what you don't want, have you succeeded or have you failed?"

Can you in any way relate?

When find yourself boohooing about your latest disappointment, you may have decided too soon what that experience really means. It could actually be the best thing to ever happen to you; just give it a minute. That's the key to reframing your failure.

Because most of us are mistaken about what failure truly is, here are few reminders of what failure is *not*:

- Failure is not being unsure of the answer or what to do;
- Failure is not experiencing criticism or being imperfect;
- Failure is not the fact that you're afraid;
- Failure is not realizing you need help.

And, as you will see in a moment, failure is often not. . . failure.

Return on Failure Tip No. 2: Get Over It—Fast

Failure isn't always an indication of being off-purpose; it's sometimes a result of poor decision-making, lack of preparation or inefficient investment. In short—you screwed up. The screw-up is fact, and how long you take to get over that fact determines the magnitude of its impact.

Older people have a way of putting things into perspective quickly, and one of my mentors, Rosemary, whom I playfully nicknamed my "Oracle," invited me over one night to chat about why I had been in an emotional funk for weeks. As Rosemary began to ask questions, I realized I had bottled up so much shame from what I felt like were major failures in my business—poor decisions, wasted resources, wasted time, second-guessing. I had tried for months to reframe those failures because some of those disappointments were indeed indescribable gifts in my life. But for some reason, I still had this unrelenting whisper in my spirit that taunted me. "You're a fake," it would say. "Who are you trying to fool? Look how you screwed everything up."

I was explaining this to Rosemary when she pointed out bluntly, "Game over. In the business of life, you win some and you lose some. You lost. Get over it."

What? I lost?

It seems like the simplest of realities, but it was a major breakthrough for me. I understand that in head-to-head competition, there can only be one winner. Sometimes you're that winner, other times you're not; it's just the way it goes. For some reason, though, I viewed going after my big dreams very differently. I thought I was in a race all by myself, performing for an audience of one, and the only person who could keep me from succeeding at the dream was me. Clearly, I had bought into the "master of my fate, captain of my soul" dogma pretty hard.

I had been deliberate, I sought advice, I followed direction, I took big risks, I stepped through fear, I made unimaginable sacrifices. But as Bruce Wilkinson wrote in the book, "The Dream Giver," "sometimes when you risk everything, you lose everything, too. Or so it seems at the time." Bruce must have been onto something because, at one point, I had dropped from earning six-figures to needing my parents' help to pay my bills.

I had lost everything… or so it seemed at the time.

The problem with me losing is I had attached *losing* with *loser*. I had placed so much personal judgment on losing that it took me way too long to accept I had lost. I knew intellectually I had failed, that I had made mistakes, but I couldn't grasp that failure was okay. Because I couldn't grasp that failing was *okay*, I spent too much time repairing my ego instead of confidently assessing what happened and quickly making my next move.

Yep, I lost a boatload of money. Yep, the first couple of businesses failed. Just as a championship team loses a lot of games on the road to winning the big one, losing is par for the course for bodacious living! I could make more money. I could try the business again. I could do something altogether different. Whatever I did, I first needed to get the hell over it—fast.

Return on Failure Tip No. 3: Stay Flexible

Unless you have been living under a rock for the past 20, 30 or 40 years, you've noticed by now that life never goes according to plan. Benjamin figured that out early in life:

"I grew up as one of seven kids. If you've come from a big family or know someone from a big family, flexibility is the norm. There's no such thing as a plan. The plan is constantly changing. Your needs and desires are often put to the backburner for the group's needs and desires. You may think, 'Oh, we're going to do this today.' But you wake up, and three of the seven kids are sick. So you're not going to do that today. You just learn you're going to do something different and adjust accordingly."

Somewhere on the Autobahn to success, many people lose that flexibility. You get so fixated on your one brilliant plan that you can't possibly imagine there is another way to accomplish your goal. You can't conceive of the fact that the deal didn't go through or that the hiring manager didn't choose you or that prospective new love didn't love you back. You're saying to yourself, "But this is *me!* Can't you see how awesome I am?"

Real estate investor, Tony, put it like this:

"Yes or no doesn't tell me who I am, it simply tells me where to go. Okay, this person said no… then how about the next person? Having the ability to move left or right, backward or forward, will determine whether or not I get what I want."

> ## Conversations in the Fast Lane
>
> ✓ If you reframed a particular failure in your life, how would that change how you move forward?
>
> ✓ How good are you at getting over personal or professional letdowns?
>
> ✓ Are you more rigid or flexible when it comes to getting what you want out of life, and how does that affect how you process failure?
>
> ✓ What kind of return have you been getting on the inevitable failures in your life? Have you become more open and free or more withdrawn and guarded as a result?

Exactly. A closed door is never the end; it is always, always, always the beginning. It can be the beginning of a new direction you never would have considered had you not walked the flames of failure, and it may be the absolute perfect direction for you. It can be the beginning of a comeback, and who ever tires of the latest "Rocky" story?

I'm a capitalist at heart, and I often tell my clients that from your pain comes your profit. It's exactly what happened with the late Apple CEO Steve Jobs. If you have not heard his 2005 Stanford commencement address, I highly recommend you do a little Googling. Jobs said, in part:

"I had just turned 30, and then I got fired. How can you get fired from a company you started? Well, as Apple grew we hired someone who I thought was very talented to run the company with me, and for the first year or so things went well. But then our visions of the future began to diverge, and eventually we had a falling out. When we did, our board of directors sided with him. So at 30 I was out. And very publicly out. What had been the focus of my entire adult life was gone, and it was devastating…

"I didn't see it then, but it turned out that getting fired from Apple was the best thing that could have ever happened to me. The heaviness of being successful was replaced by the lightness of being a beginner again, less sure about everything. It freed me to enter one of the most creative periods of my life."

Jobs would start other companies, including NeXT and Pixar, and eventually returned to lead Apple. That "creative period" led to the resurgence of the company with the invention of the iPod, iPhone, iPad—products people are so fanatical about today.

The same will happen for you—maybe in a different magnitude—but the principle is the same. I have learned that from your pain often comes your passion, from your frustration comes your future, and in your angst you will find your authentic self. Do not avoid failure; just get good at using it to your advantage.

"We can negotiate with ourselves until our bodies say, 'Enough!' I used to get I.V. transfusions for iron. I would go in with chemo patients and have transfusions for two hours… I haven't had a transfusion since I left my company."

— Veronica, attorney

CHAPTER 10

••••

Busted Body

FIBROIDS. ACID REFLUX. Insomnia. Bronchitis. Acne. Depression. Panic attacks. Cloudy thinking. Exhaustion. Back pain. Indigestion. Heartburn. Teeth grinding. Mental breakdown. Obesity. Substance abuse. Binge eating. Migraines. High blood pressure. Forgetfulness. Weight gain.

What do all of these ailments have in common? 1.) They're avoidable, and 2.) they are so prevalent among fast-laners that it is likely you suffer from one or more them. Speeding through life at 70 percent of mental and physical capacity is normal, but it's not natural. Many of us are able to mask the effects a fast lane lifestyle has on our bodies through a shot of caffeine or the sedation of a glass of wine. But as Veronica said in the opening quote, you can negotiate with your body for only so long.

> "I was going at a fast pace in the seemingly right direction, but I wasn't taking the time to heed the warning signs. I kept pushing through sickness because of fear. My company was cutting people during the dot-com bust. I had been working on a project for a year when I tore the ligament in my knee. I needed surgery but I kept thinking I couldn't afford not to be chargeable, so I worked through the pain. I didn't take the physical therapy, and when I eventually did, it took three months to heal instead of the initial two to three weeks. Psychologically and emotionally, I think it took me three months because my body didn't want to go back; my body literally wouldn't heal. I was burned out."
>
> — *Teresa, business consulting manager*

If you're currently in the fast lane going in the wrong direction, there's no doubt you can relate to this in some way. Granted, no one sets out to destroy their body by any means necessary, but the unwillingness to rest and care for yourself sets up a domino effect that ultimately diminishes your quality of life. Notice I said the *unwillingness* to rest (not the inability to) is jacking you up—big time.

We have all kinds of reasons we're choosing to self-destruct, but regardless of the reason, we still suffer the consequences of our decisions in our body and we must own to that. It's not okay to have bronchitis every six months. It's not okay to pop antacids like they're Skittles. It's not okay to wake up nearly as tired as when you went to bed the night before.

It's not okay.

The common fast-lane adage, "I can sleep when I'm dead," may come sooner than you realize. That comment feeds our ego, but it is neither realistic nor sustainable. The last thing any of us are thinking when we are faced with a diabetes or cancer diagnosis is, "I can sleep when I'm dead." Just ask some of our business and professional icons who have battled life-threatening illnesses, many of which were brought on by decades of hard-charging mistreatment of their bodies.

No one else is in position to say what you should do when it comes to your health because each person is different. But I will demonstrate how your busted body is moving you farther from everything you're striving so hard to achieve. Consider: When you picture the fast-lane rock star you believe you should be, does he or she look like the person staring back at you in the mirror?

I was working for a consulting firm on assignment for a client in San Francisco and making great money for a 20-something. I had a swanky apartment with an amazing view of the Golden Gate Bridge, paid for by the client. On the outside, life was good—real good. On the inside, I could not have been more dispassionate and disengaged. By that point, I had gritted through a few compounded years of passionless living that, unknown to me, were coming to a head of depression.

One radiantly sunny day during that assignment, I was meandering through downtown San Francisco at lunch, doing what looked on the surface like relaxed window shopping. In actuality, that stroll was a desperate attempt to mentally escape before going back to work. I happened to catch the reflection of a young woman in a storefront glass. Her hair was pulled back in a frumpy ponytail. She was frail, dowdy with gray dress slacks and a black blouse that both looked a size too big. Quite honestly, she looked a tired mess.

As if snapping out of a trance, my eyes focused, and I was shocked to realize that frail, dowdy, frumpy, tired woman in the reflection was *me!* I will never forget it because my dull, dragging reflection was in stark contrast to the unusually bright, sunny day and the fast-paced bustle of the people around me.

No matter how I had rationalized things before, the woman in the mirror confirmed all was not well in my world. I had known this truth for months, but I honestly did not understand how I could be "checking all the boxes" professionally and still feel so dejected. Something must be *wrong* with me. Something was wrong, all right, but at the time, I still didn't fully get the message. I had a chronic fatigue diagnosis, digestive disorders and a yearlong bout of mono still to come before I got a clue.

What does the man (or woman) in the mirror say about you? Not the made-up version of you, but the version of you before it gets "retouched" by the photographer, before it gets the Starbucks boost, before it downs another margarita? Without self-care (physical, mental and emotional), you'll either have crazy coping mechanisms like caffeine, drugs and sugar, or you won't be able to manage at all.

So choose. Either get high on addictive stuff or get healthy. You must do one or the other if you want to reach your goal. One ends in vitality; the other in a sickly life— or early death.

What Are You Missing?

I can do without alcohol, I absolutely hate the smell of coffee, I'm not a caffeine drinker nor am I super addicted to sugar. That's good, because I've likely spared myself even greater damage than I realize. But avoiding the common coping vices meant my body really *felt* the effects of my lifestyle—with no buffers!

I suffered chronic fatigue for years, feeling the lack of energy, focus and mental clarity when I was out of balance. I wouldn't sleep enough. I wouldn't eat enough. I wouldn't hydrate enough. I didn't know how to just relax, yet I drove myself like a workhorse.

When I first started making changes to my diet, I had a personal affirmation that said, "Nothing tastes as good as vitality feels," to remind me to make healthier eating choices. I couldn't figure out why that did absolutely nothing for me. I wasn't any more motivated to stave off the ice cream and macaroni and cheese than I was before. I realized it was because I didn't actually *know* what vitality felt like. I had been tired for years, literally, so everything tasted better than vitality felt because I had no vivacity!

It took me a while, but it finally dawned on me that everything I ever wanted in life— success, great relationships and, yes, even great sex— hinges on how well I take care of myself. I've grown to be a pretty big believer in abstinence outside of marriage (that's a topic for another book), but I'm also a firm believer of a lot of sex within marriage, and I look forward to it (perish the thought if my daddy has read this far into the book!). Anyway, it's commonly recognized that good health is a huge contributor to a healthy sex drive, so, admittedly, that was a huge motivator for me to change.

I also considered I would likely have kids later in life, and the pure exhaustion I notice with 40-something parents of young children was not attractive to me. I want the vitality to enjoy my kids, and I don't want to experience that through the lens of chronic fatigue.

> ## Conversations in the Fast Lane
>
> ✓ Take a moment, get quiet and actually <u>feel</u> what your body is revealing? Are you tired? Chronic aches and pains? Are you mentally foggy? What is the "man in the mirror" saying that you need to change now?
>
> ✓ What coping mechanisms are you using to mask what's really going on with your mind and body? Is it working?
>
> ✓ Are there any excuses you have been telling yourself to justify neglecting to take impeccable care of yourself? How long has that been going on?
>
> ✓ What you are missing because you're not physically and mentally 100 percent? Are you missing out on relationships with your kids, significant other or other meaningful experiences?
>
> ✓ If you did a complete turnaround in your health, what would change for you—in your relationship or marriage, parenting, income, productivity, fulfillment?

Whether I'm motivated by sex or the prospect of kids, the reality is I am more creative when I'm rested, hydrated and healthy. I have brighter ideas. I enjoy people more. I get things done faster and am more productive. I experience so much more of life when I'm not in a fog.

What about you?

What in life are you missing because you choose the fast lane over taking care of your body? We often think if we just push through this next season of our life, hit the big goal or reach a steady state in our business, we'll have time to regroup. That is so untrue. You may attain the goal, but if you can't experience the joy of the achievement, what have you really gained? And who would truly be impressed?

So here's the question: At what point will you raise your standards and begin to *be* the part instead of *look* the part—complete with the energy, vitality and mental clarity you deserve?

What does that mean, practically? The answer varies for different people, but here are two challenges:

First, take impeccable care of your body. I didn't say take good care of your body; I said take impeccable care. Fuel it, nourish it, hydrate it, rejuvenate it and clean it from the inside out, regularly. Healthy maintenance of your body is the one area of your life that has guaranteed positive returns.

Second, take one day a week to *completely* shut off work.

When I was at the early stages of writing this book, I had a random conversation with my mechanic, Gili, as he picked me up to service my car. I admire Gili's success with his auto shop. In eight years, he had developed a thriving business, opened a new auto body shop next door and generated enough customer base to pay off the loan on the auto body shop in just two years. He had a number of very competent technicians working for him, and he had a lot of free time on his hands. . . so much so that he was hard-pressed to find something to do with his time.

Always searching for best practices for this book, I asked him to share two or three secrets to his success. Aside from making the investments to hire the right people, he said:

> *I VOWED NEVER to work on Saturdays, and I left for home by 6 p.m., even if there was more work to do or more money to be made.*

When I asked what *not* working on Saturdays did for him, he said:
It was oxygen. Pure oxygen.

You might think it's easy for Gili since he owns his own business and sets his own hours, but what if you're a mom with kids or you're working a stressful job where people depend on you?

My friend Andrea Moore is a women's ministry leader with three children, and she shared the concept of her book, *God Took a Day Off, Why Can't I: How to Exert Less Effort and Produce Greater Results*. She chooses one day a week to completely shut down. For Andrea, that day is not Sunday, as those days can feel more like a full workday than a day of rest.

She makes arrangements for the children, she doesn't take calls, doesn't run errands. Instead, she uses that time to connect with herself, with God, or do absolutely nothing. Her husband supports that effort and helps to create that environment for her and has taken on the practice for himself. As her three young boys are getting older, they are now being conditioned to slow down, as well, on a day the family calls "Terrific Tuesdays." For Andrea, it's not a matter of hiring a babysitter to offload the kids; it's a matter of training the kids to shut down on that day, too. She's setting boundaries.

"I think the common trait of many people is they are very lonely, and you find big cities full of these lonely people ."

— Nathan King, founder of *SoulNeeds.com*

CHAPTER 11
••••
It's All About Who You Know

I LOVE NATHAN'S opening quote because it confirms that the challenges I notice with fast-lane relationships here in the United States also transcend countries and continents. Empty, shallow, superficial relationships are a universal problem. Who knew? You knew.

Thanks to the Internet and social media, we come in contact with more people on a weekly basis than ever, yet many of us feel more disconnected and isolated. Single people often dismiss the disconnection, because they assume it will change when they get married. But the truth is unless you change how you approach relationships in general, you'll feel equally lonely when you are married. I can't speak to marriage from personal experience, but that reality is confirmed over and over by my married clients.

This chapter addresses relationships in general: friendships, networking and connections. In the next chapter, we look at "Fast Lane in Love." What you take from this chapter, however, will challenge and coach you on how to deal with your more intimate relationships, so avoid the temptation to skip through this one just to get to the juicy stuff.

Tier One Relationships

Over the years, I have found we encounter three tiers of relationships. First, there are those who look up to you. It's really hard to be honest and open with this crowd because they think you're oh-so-great, and to reveal your less-than-stellar side to them would devalue your stock in the marketplace of public adulation. I had one client say, "I don't want to disappoint so-and-so; they really think I'm awesome."

With the exception of the occasional gold-digging family member, this group often places less value on your achievements than you may think. They believe you are so freakin' amazing that when you express fears, doubts or failures, they're almost relieved to know you're actually a part of the human race like everyone else. This group is often the most encouraging because what you are accomplishing in life is so far beyond their imagination that they are your biggest cheerleaders. They believe you can achieve *anything,* even though they are often clueless about what exactly you do.

When you're down and out, this is not the "dust-yourself-off-and-get back-in-the-game!" crew; they are the ones who rejuvenate you when you're burned out and admonish you to take it easy, something most fast-laners can hardly conceive on their own.

Tier Two Relationships

This group of people are your peers—those like you who are also moving and shaking. You respect them and their accomplishments, but you still have confidence you might be able to "take 'em" if it came down to a battle of who is worth more. At a minimum, it would be a close contest.

The fear around this crew is if you show vulnerability, they might discover you are a phony and not good enough to be a part of the fast-lane clique. It's with this tier that the "Fraud Syndrome" in chapter 3 most commonly shows up. As a business owner, when I recount the many times I failed or how long it took me to get to a certain level of success, there were times I felt embarrassed. I used to think, "I should have taken over the world by now!"

In the throes of the building process, I would question, "If it's taking me this long, can I really cut the mustard?" Or, "If it's taking me this long to figure out how to become happy, what's wrong with me?" While there are always exceptions, you won't typically share those inner thoughts with your Tier Two peers. And you're definitely not going to share them with Tier One relationships, because without Tier Ones, your ego would be shot to pieces, for sure.

Tier Three Relationships

This last group consists of the senior execs, mentors, gurus, icons or simply wildly successful people that you *feel* are so far out of your league. They may not be that much further along in life than you, but the standard of their life challenges and intimidates you. As a result, you spend more time trying to impress them with who you are and what you know. When you are around them, you fail to actually connect and learn from them.

All of these relationship tiers are vital to your growth, success and overall fulfillment, yet most of us will admit an imbalance in the ratio and quality of these relationships. Moreover, you may notice that while you have three tiers of relationships, you are likely not open and vulnerable with any of them, and therein is a fundamentally big problem.

Cultivating these relationships is not as simple as deciding to add more people to each bucket. You have to make three very important decisions to change how you show up as an individual. These decisions are simple, but in no way easy.

Decision No. 1: Check Your Motives

When it comes to relationships, you must decide on the company you keep based on who you are and what you value in your life, not based on how someone could "advance" your life. Far too often, fast-laners maintain relationships with people they don't like or respect because they're "good people to know" for connections. Sometimes you have people in your business or personal circle because you fear you can't succeed without them. However, what commonly occurs is you build relationships just to see what you can get out of them with little to no consideration of what you can bring to them or the quality of the characters with whom you're dealing.

> **"Relationships were very transactional, very superficial.
> You create rapport to get what you need."**
> — *Terry, consultant*

> **"Fast lane, wrong direction in relationships becomes like a business. In business, you only deal with people who are going to help you move up the next rung."**
> — *Craig, investor*

> **"I was not very good at being social.
> People were not serving me in business, so I couldn't use them."**
> — *Andrew, entrepreneur*

Don't misunderstand—I'm a big proponent of being strategic in how you build relationships. We are a reflection of the people we spend the most time with, so if you want high-quality people in your circle of influence, actively build with high-quality people. But go headlong into those relationships as a *giver*. Do not use people solely for your personal gain. Instead, make a conscious decision to be an over-the-top contributor in that relationship, however intimate or casual the relationship might be. That doesn't mean you should be a "brown-noser," but it does mean you actively consider how you can add value to that person's life professionally, personally and otherwise.

Whom can you connect *them* with? What resource can *you* provide? How can you support *their* goals? That decision alone will have people bending over backwards to help you when you need help the most. On the flip side, do not violate your integrity or values, or allow the other party to disrespect you. In these cases, you will regret having compromised yourself.

When the real estate market collapsed, Clay started a new business brokering deals with underperforming mortgages and bank-owned properties. His story says volumes:

> **"ALL I WAS** concerned with on a daily basis was how many deals I could evaluate, the profit margin of the transaction and the fees associated with me brokering the deal. When you are dealing in any distressed market, vultures prey on that market. People come in who don't have good intentions and want to take advantage. The vast majority of the people that were in that space were not people I would normally deal with, but I gave no thought to that. I was deal-focused, not people-focused.
>
> That was until my business ceased to be a business. I was using the same strategies I had used in the past, working just as hard, but the business was failing and I couldn't do anything to make it stop. It made me think, 'This is really odd. There's something going on that's larger than me.' There was no reason why out of the hundreds of deals I was being presented with, none of them were closing. That created a shift in my thinking.
>
> Looking back, I didn't compromise my personal values, necessarily, but I never considered the background of the people with whom I was doing the deal. In my new space of life, I want to know more about what's going on with you, your children, your goals—personally or professionally. I am more people-focused as opposed to deal-focused, and I won't do business with you if our values don't line up.
>
> It is the single most important decision I've made in my life outside of marrying my wife. It has literally changed my life. It has changed my business and people's perceptions of me. The internal profit is infinite; the financial profit can't be measured. If you focus on the quality of your relationships as opposed to just deal flow and profit, you have a much greater likelihood of doing substantive work. You may not assess as many opportunities, but they'll be the right opportunities and better opportunities. **"**

Author Wayne Dyer once said, "Treat every person you meet like a holy encounter." If you keep in mind every person you meet is valuable but you don't *need* any single person, you avoid building relationships triggered by fear or other destructive motivations.

Decision No. 2: Get Real

"My friends think I'm an open book. If people closest to me would take notice, they'd realize I tell them very little about what's really going on in my heart. I don't tell them anything real, like how I don't feel self-actualized, how I don't feel like I have a lot to offer to a life partner."

—*Amber, senior director*

There was a time when Amber's comment could have been a page out of my journal. It takes tremendous courage and inner strength to get to a place where you practice transparency, but it is one of the most important skills you can acquire. It's scary because you leave yourself vulnerable to get your feelings hurt by someone else's ego trips, by their judgment, rejection or mistreatment of you in some way.

But when you choose the freedom of living that way, your relationships become so much more meaningful, and you actually make more money, open yourself to more opportunities and generate more success. People are attracted to you because you are a person of substance, and that substance draws out the uniqueness and realness of others.

My friend Joey shared an encounter he had with the woman eventually married:

"BERIT AND I had known each other for several years. We worked in the same office and lived across the street from each other. I was walking her home one night [as friends] and she said, 'I feel like I have to put in an application to be your friend.'

"'What do you mean by that?'" I asked.

She explained, 'You're really good friends with one of my business partners and one of my employees, and they seem to have a depth of understanding of you I'm not familiar with. I'd be curious to know what the real you is like. I think there's the you the rest of the world sees, but I feel like one has to put in an application to see what the real you is like.'

I had been thinking that maybe my façade wasn't as good as I thought it was, and that conversation with Berit was confirmation."

This story is as much about Berit as Joey. Berit has a standard for how she shows up in relationships—authentic and real—and she transfers that standard to the people she allows in her life. There is no room to play in Berit's sandbox if you can't first take off your "everything-is-all-good" mask.

Of course, this doesn't mean you tell every person you meet your deepest, darkest secrets, but it does mean you get beyond the surface and begin to live so much more honestly with your dreams, fears and hurdles. That is what endears people to you.

I know Joey personally, and he has invested a lot of time, money and resources into his personal growth to be secure in himself and more transparent. The transformation he has made within himself has completely revolutionized how he views relationships and the authenticity he demands from other people in his circle. The following depiction of how Joey raised his standards brilliantly illustrates the point of Decision No. 2.

"I was always willing to share my dreams and ambitions; I was not so willing to share my fears or my worries," Joey said. "However, the more I play at what is typically seen as a higher echelon of power, society or accomplishment, the more willing I am to have these types of conversations with people. I notice that people in those positions willingly admit they're regularly anxious, regularly scared, that they regularly doubt. If all of us could come to the table with that at the outset instead of playing the games where we pretend nothing fazes us, that we're okay working 100-hour work weeks or missing yet another family event, an entirely new world would open up.

"I go to networking events now, and I'm not interested in, 'So what do you do?' Or, 'How was your weekend?' I'm into, 'So tell me about the most fascinating place you've been in your life.' Or, 'What are you most excited about for the year?' You suddenly have a completely different conversation. You're pushing into the conversation that needs to happen and wants to happen instead of the conversation everyone thinks 'should' happen.

"When you go to the next networking event and someone asks you, 'How are you doing?' remember this advice and wait for the magic moment when somebody says, 'Wow, I haven't had this type of conversation at a networking event in a long time.'"

Oooh... *goose pimples!*

I truly believe the world opens when we change the way we connect with people. When we are on purpose with our life, when we feel we don't have to put on airs, we are self-assured whether we are on-track, off-track or trying to find a track. We can be in the place of truth, not worrying about what we should say but focusing only on what is being said.

Decision No. 3: Prioritize Staying Connected

I realize it is hard to foster relationships with all that competes for your time. As a single person, I find it challenging, and, no doubt, it's even more complicated for married people or someone with kids. But it is essential and totally possible to cultivate our connections when we condition ourselves to focus on the activities and priorities that grant us the highest return on fulfillment.

If you've ever tracked how you spend your time each day, you may find you spend a lot of it on "empty calorie activities," such as idle chatter at the water cooler, excessive time on the Internet and email, daydreaming and escaping, or mindless phone conversations that add little to no value to your overall growth and happiness. Choose to stop that and replace it by investing that time, however short at the start, in relationships that will progress you.

Remember the three tiers of relationships we talked about at the beginning of the chapter? Let's revisit them because each is vital to maintaining fast lane, right direction in our lives, yet the majority of us have a major imbalance.

Conversations in the Fast Lane

✓ Take inventory of your relationships. What is your overall proportion of Tier One, Two and Three relationships? Is there an imbalance anywhere?

✓ Do you need more low-key relationships that help you take off the mask and simply enjoy life? By low-key, I'm not talking boring, I'm talking life-enriching. That could mean more downtime or more wild and crazy adventures.

✓ With your Tier Two relationships, are you being called higher? What's your personal standard for authenticity, realness and growth? What expectation do you have for how other people show up for you? Do these relationships foster an open spirit where you can talk about your weaknesses and fears? Are these the people who provide input into your next career and business moves, and are you doing the same for them?

✓ Do you strategically schedule time in your calendar to talk with your Tier Two relationships at least twice a month, even if only a quick call?

✓ What Tier Three relationships would totally advance your personal, career or business goals? Have you invested in that person's program, seminar or association, productivity, fulfillment?

> "When I started building my business, I lost friends. There's a part of you that has to go into the cave to create, but you do have to be able to balance the time you have with your friends and family with the time you use to create the business because those are the people who knew you when."
>
> — Melanie, entrepreneur

For entrepreneurs, in particular, there is a part of you that does go into a cave if you're launching a new project or coming up to speed in mastery. This also happens for careerists when the learning curve is steep or you're stepping up to a new role. Whatever the circumstance, you must make a commitment to yourself to stay connected to people. If you don't, you'll suffer for the disengagement. You'll suffer with the most intimate relationships and friendships that ultimately make life more enriching, and you will also stifle your professional progress.

Doors are opened by *relationships*. Your path is made smoother by *relationships*. One referral call by an acquaintance who is friends with a new prospect can be the difference between you landing a contract and the next person getting it. How many times have you been banging your head against the wall on a personal or professional problem only to talk with a friend who had the solution… in 10 minutes?!

How many times have you been pushed to the next level because one of your friends was living their life at a higher standard? It's the *relationship*. And these relationships aren't fostered overnight. You can't just decide to pick up the phone when you need somebody. You must invest along the way, so be very strategic about scheduling these encounters into your life.

Your success and the speed with which you attain that success are not solely dependent upon your skill; it is largely dependent on your relationships. There are plenty of not-so-bright people who are doing extraordinary things because of the relationships they keep. Beyond that, successful people who are most balanced and fulfilled are those who have developed rich relationships with which to enjoy the spoils of life.

When people nail the relationship component, somehow life becomes so much sweeter.

CHAPTER 12
····
Fast Lane in Love

IF YOU HAVE read this far, you likely recognized how often the following questions surface in the life of a fast-laner: "Will I be loved?" and "Am I enough?" These questions are certainly at the root of our insecurities in career, business and friendships, yet there is no place where these questions are more prevalent than in our intimate relationships.

You could speak before a crowd of thousands, perform open-heart surgery or rescue a kid from a burning building, yet still struggle to confidently go out on a first date or believe after years of marriage you're finally good enough for your wife. Funny how the dearest thing to our hearts (love) can be the most elusive and crippling to our spirits…

… but that's love in the fast lane.

Finding and keeping love is a universal, daily struggle for many people, and as fast-laners, when we do anything, we do it BIG! Screwing ourselves (figuratively) in relationships is no different. We have a way of bringing conventional rules of success, which we often have wrong in the first place, into the heart space. That usually results in a royal—and often expensive—mess because not only do fast-laners fail to do things small, we also rarely do things cheap. Love is no great exception.

So, in the concept of "fast lane in love," there are three questions you must consider:

1.) Who Do You Believe You Are?

"I don't feel like I have a lot to offer to a partner. I'm unhappy and unfulfilled. I wouldn't date me, so I give my number to people I would never date. I get hit on by 20-somethings, and I give my number to them. To the 40-year old who has got it all together, I'm not together. I don't want to date someone who could judge me, because I have less of a shot of disappointing them."

— *Jillian, chief operating officer*

That is a quote worth repeating from chapter 3. Would you believe the biggest deterrent for people in relationships is they don't believe they're good enough for a relationship, even if they're *in* one? They don't feel thin enough, wealthy enough, "degreed" enough, stable enough or secure enough. Those beliefs affect how they select their partner, as well as how they manage the relationship, whether they are married or dating.

The irony is, being good enough is never, ever, ever a function of who or what you are on the outside. Sure, you may want to lose some weight or gain some weight, fix your credit, build your business or do a host of other things. I'm all for creating a "brand new super you," but if you don't believe you're already enough in the midst of the transformation, you'll never be enough after the transformation; you'll simply replace the original deficiency with something else.

Nobody wants anybody whose insecurities suck the life out of the relationship, whether directly or indirectly. Everybody wants somebody who brings life *to* the relationship. (*Disclaimer:* I am assuming we're talking about healthy relationships, not the co-dependent, dysfunctional or gold-digging ones that require completely different selection criteria.)

Let's face it—we're all a "work in progress." One person might have the killer body but feel less-than in their accomplishments. Another is a rock star in the boardroom and a Little Debbie groupie in the kitchen. You're not the only one with problems. You're not the only one with "unpresentable" parts, and no matter how down on yourself you might be at times, there's always someone else who'll beat you for the "I Suck Award."

It's time to get over your woe.

Whether you are counseled through it, coached through it or pray through it, you must decide to do what it takes to get over this self-worthlessness, no matter what. Authentic confidence might not be easy, but it must be done. *No,* I don't know your situation. *No,* I don't know your past, and none of that matters if it keeps you from your future.

Have you considered that the person you date or marry is going to have "unpresentable" parts of his or her own—emotionally, physically or otherwise, and the only way you can have grace for their shortcomings is to figure out a way to have grace for your own?

Just because a mate doesn't want you doesn't mean you're not good enough. Just because you're on the road to a better version of yourself doesn't mean you're not good enough as you are. It's a paradox, I know, and in some ways it's a chicken-and-egg argument.

But quality, fulfilling relationships hinge on you knowing this as *fact*—even if there is no one around you to reinforce it as true. If you miss this point, you will find yourself in the fast lane going in the wrong direction on the first date, 10 months into the relationship, going down the aisle, or five years after you've said, "I do."

Got it?

2.) How Do You Choose?

"When you're in the fast lane going in the wrong direction and your mental and physical state is off, your decision-making is also off. So, choosing to embark on a relationship at a time when you're unstable is not going to make for a healthy relationship."

—Pamela, IT consultant

When we find ourselves in the wrong direction of any area of our lives, we are blind to just how deficient our judgment has become, especially in love. Everything else is spinning around you at break-neck speed and you try to find solace or control or meaning in another person. A relationship will never fill a void elsewhere in your life, and a bigger problem is that "fast lane in love" often has a terribly flawed selection compass that can lead to a very unhealthy and dissatisfying union.

> I didn't think about what I wanted in a wife. I don't mean in a "make-a-list" sort of way. I didn't consider what I needed in my essence and character, nor did I consider what I could give or provide to have a relationship filled with joy, love, a sense of trust and kindness. In my rush for companionship, I don't think I was deliberate enough in those considerations.
>
> — Emerson, politician

As we read in Emerson's comments, when fast lane wants love, it often wants it *now, now, now, now, now!* Sometimes, people have deferred pursuing relationships for so many years that when the urge for connection awakens, it rears with a vengeance to make up for lost time, to keep up with the Joneses or to satisfy the thirst for genuine love and connection that has gone unquenched for so long. In those moments, all that matters is what's the fastest way to *done*. Fast-laners know how to get things done fast, though we might not always get them done right. And getting it wrong in relationships usually comes with a fairly hefty price.

Sometimes love in the fast lane must measure up to a performance review of qualities comprised of looks, pedigree, FICO score, fraternity affiliation, economic status, appearance and a whole host of factors to ensure the union shines brightly in the marketplace of public opinion. In and of themselves, these factors are neither good nor bad. The problem lies when we check off external factors because they satisfy our egos without considering the weightier elements of character.

Who is that person at the core? What do they value? Do their values align with mine? Am I a better person at my core because of this other person? Do they call me to be my best, to contribute more and be more productive to the world around me or do I become more self-focused, more insecure and shallow? Do I feel safe to fail with this person? Am I safe to be afraid? Who is this person when their beauty, success and status are threatened? Does the strength of their character rise, or do they become uglier in spirit? Am I truly joyful and alive with this person or am I merely a shell of happiness? These types of questions must become part of the selection criteria for choosing a lover that enriches us, but many of us don't even consider the questions because we're afraid of what the answers reveal about us.

Other times, fast-laners are so burned out that the determining factor for staying in a relationship is whether or not they can get all the benefits of companionship without the responsibility of the bond. My friend Jacob from Australia shared his philosophy on "chick picks" when he was in the fast lane going in the wrong direction:

> *I WENT FOR women who wouldn't give me grief. I didn't want to know about their problems. I didn't want to connect to other people at a deeper level because that was too much for me to handle.*

Have you ever had those seasons in your life where you were just tired? Not just tired for a day, but tired for months, and you simply didn't have the emotional energy to deal with conflict or compromise? Trust me, those are *not* the seasons to go looking for a new fling. Your selection compass will be way off, and you'll end up using another person physically, emotionally and otherwise. It's more drama than it's worth. If you're unwilling to progress toward the "right direction" for your life during that season, don't scoop up an unsuspecting passenger for the ride. It's totally and completely unfair, and it will come back to bite you when you least expect it.

On the flip side, if you're in the wrong direction, you really must carefully consider your decision to maintain or end a relationship. The level of overwhelm that comes from being exhausted, insecure, fearful and emotionally busted does not make for sound decision-making on matters of the heart. When your primal desire is to get out of the pain your fast lane choices have caused, it can distort your perception of your mate, their intentions toward you, and what you think you want from them.

You might say, "This woman is the problem; she's stressing me out," or "I just need a man who meets my needs." For some, that results in ending relationships too prematurely with the expectation that the grass is greener on the other side. No, the grass isn't greener; you just don't have the emotional energy to mow your own daggone lawn!

Still, for others, the lack of emotional and physical capacity associated with the fast lane keeps them in relationships far longer than they should, because it's a lot easier to deal with the status quo than with the stress and discomfort of a much-needed split.

As you can see, there's no universal answer, and the purpose of this section is to prompt you to consider how being fast lane-wrong direction might be affecting the choices you make in love—the choice to stay, the choice to go and everything in between. I encourage you to be honest and open with the person you're in a relationship with, but I highly recommend taking a step back to fix *you* first before making decisions that affect another person's heart.

This is why taking care of our health—our body and our emotional well-being—is so vitally important. Dealing with relationships can be difficult because of the emotional energy required of them. When we're exhausted and mentally drained, we'll plow through work deadlines and make sure the family's physical and material needs are taken care of… but we'll shove relationship issues under the bus so quickly it'll make the other person's head spin. But those issues don't dissipate, they magnify.

3.) How Do You Show Up?

"My marriage was traditional: go to work, bring home the bacon, don't bother me, I want some dinner, I want some sex," said Craig, an investor. "If I didn't experience getting those things, I'd just go to work more. The connection is what I wanted, but I thought that if you work hard and take care of your wife, that stuff would be automatic. As it didn't happen that way, I'd get more upset. So, you start to trade in a marriage. I'll take you to dinner or buy you something to get the connection. As a society, we barter and buy love and attention through our acts instead of just being present all the time, instead of looking at how we can be a contribution to someone else's life and realizing that as they get what they want in their life, we get what we want.

"THE TURNING POINT was when my wife said she was leaving me," Craig continued. "I was sideswiped. Things weren't great between us, but I thought we were normal. I loved her, but I didn't like her; she was on my nerves. I wanted something that I wasn't getting, and I didn't know how to express it. I was working and giving her what she wanted, but I didn't feel fulfilled in the relationship. I was holding her responsible for all of that rather than myself. I realized it wasn't her responsibility, it was mine. I went from caring about what she said (or didn't say) to validate me, to knowing within myself that I was a good man, a great husband and a great father."

I don't know much about marriage, but I do know about horsetrading in relationships and doing stuff with the expectation of getting something in return. When we show up that way in relationships—marriage, dating or otherwise—we are guaranteed to be disappointed. In the fast lane of career or business, our actions typically generate a result, and most of us will cease the action if we don't reap the results in sufficient time. Relationships are never about fairness and reciprocity, and when we bring that mentality into our intimate relationships, we suffer on a broad level, as Craig learned.

> ## Conversations in the Fast Lane
>
> ✓ If you reflect on your most painful or disappointing relationship, did you grow into a better, freer version of yourself or devolve into a more guarded, restrained version of yourself?
>
> ✓ Did you take on any habits, mindsets or characteristics from the relationship that need to change?
>
> ✓ Are there "unpresentable" parts of you that prevent you from being completely authentic in relationships? Those parts could be physical, mental, emotional, financial, etc.
>
> ✓ Has being in the fast lane-wrong direction in any area of your life affected how you select partners in relationships? Does your selection criteria need to shift? If so, how?
>
> ✓ Do you feel free to be yourself, express yourself and give wholly of yourself in relationships without keeping score on how you're receiving in return?

· ·

How do you show up in your relationship? Is it more like a business arrangement? Do you give to get something in return? Are you keeping score on whose turn it is to do something special? Are you trying to impress or one-up your partner by your achievements? Are you holding anything back because of ego or pride?

One of the hardest things to do is to have the confidence to love, give and express yourself in a relationship independent of what we can get from the other person. How the other person responds may influence whether we stay or go, but it should never influence who we become, especially if who we become is a lesser version of our best self.

"So often, we're too busy 'doing'
to take a really critical look at ourselves because
we have to stop in order to do it."
— Lawrence, manufacturing executive

CHAPTER 13
••••
It's Okay to Take a Pit Stop

ONE WOMAN I interviewed for *Fast Lane, Wrong Direction* nailed it when she said, "Taking a rest is a pain point for fast-laners."

That's why most of us won't do it.

I'm not talking about taking a nap or a day off or even a fun-filled vacation. The rest I'm talking about is the one that allows you to stop the noise, go deep down inside, and take a good look at where your life is headed. As Lawrence said, we are often so busy, there's no time to take a critical look at ourselves. I would argue the issue isn't time; the issue is fear.

My friend Cheryl asserts, "People are afraid to ask questions, so they keep going in the wrong direction without ever questioning."

We are afraid. We're afraid of stopping and dealing with the truth of how far off we are from where we want to be. I remember having low points in my business and being afraid to open my online bank account and face the truth of how little money was there. I didn't like recording expenses or balancing a checkbook because the debits usually outweighed the credits, and it was a lot easier on the ego to be ignorant about the imbalance.

What came out of the various interviews I conducted for this book is I wasn't alone. Many people in the fast lane are afraid to take a pit stop to look under the hood of their life because so much money, time and energy has been invested in their direction, whatever that direction happens to be. But the reality is your pit stop is not optional; it's an absolute necessity. Here's why:

I love Coldstone Creamery. It is my absolute favorite ice cream shop in the world. I'll go through great inconveniences and travel distances for a scoop of their sweet concoctions. I once stood in line 45 minutes for a little cup of their cream. Most friends couldn't believe any ice cream could be so good to wait 45 minutes and, to be honest, there is no ice cream good enough for me to wait 45 minutes, at least not knowingly.

The reason I waited in line so long is I had already invested my time. When I arrived at the shop that day, there were only about 15 people ahead of me. I figured, "How long can it take?" It was a nice summer day and I had no place to be—not a problem. Ten minutes in, I had barely moved, but that was okay because in my mind, it couldn't take much longer. Twenty minutes in, the line was inching along at a snail's pace. I was a bit annoyed, for sure, but I had already invested 20 minutes of my time. If I had already spent 20 minutes in line, it would be a complete waste to leave without my ice cream. Besides, how much longer could it be?

By minute 30, I was hot, and it wasn't because of the weather. At that point, and as irritated as I had become, there was no way I was leaving that line without my cream! It was now a matter of principle.

And so it is in the fast lane.

We often know we're headed in the wrong direction, whether it's by our own design or some twist of life, as we discovered in earlier chapters. Yet in our minds we think, "How long could it possibly take?" How long could it take to make vice president of the company? How long could it take to cut my first few deals? How long could it take to get my big break?

It doesn't appear long at the start, so it seems worth the sacrifice, and maybe it is at the time. The problem comes 15 minutes (or five years) later, when we realize the business and career advancements aren't inching us any closer to what we truly want for our lives. But we rationalize, "How much longer could it be?"

How much longer could it be for me to be financially free enough to find love? How much longer could it be for me to have enough stability to live a more balanced life? How much longer could it be for me to grab the "brass ring" and walk away from this company a winner?

If anyone had told me that hot summer day it would take 45 minutes to get my ice cream, I would have hightailed it out of there. But no one told me it would take 45 minutes, and at every 10- or 15-minute interval, the time I had already invested justified just a little more sacrifice. This is exactly how five, 10 and 15 years pass by without you realizing it.

During the writing of this book, I began coaching a new client, a very accomplished woman in her 50s. She is dynamic and amazing, but her chief complaint was that work consumed her life. She had never been married, never had children, and there was an underlying fear it was too late for her. I know for a fact it is not too late for her, nor is it too late for you, but if you fail to heed the warning signs and take a pit stop to ask and answer the hard questions, it will be too late—sooner than you think.

The best way to explain the refreshment that comes in the pit stop is through the lives of some extraordinary people. Markus is a very successful entrepreneur in Europe who describes his pit stop experience:

> THE FIRST SIGN was when I got sick for about three months, but I actually didn't stop at that point. A bigger trigger happened three years ago, when I lost my last relationship. The relationship was definitely over, my health was not good and the only areas that were working were my finances and my businesses. That was the tipping point for me because I began to notice a pattern, and I could see myself repeating this scenario over and over.
>
> To get out of that spiral, I pretty much sold my business. I just stopped and moved to Spain. For me, it was like First Aid. I had to stop the poison, stop the bleeding and stop whatever I was doing. Then I worked with myself on reframing my identity. I really had to go deep down into myself and find out what I really, really wanted. I obviously had my basic needs to care for, but I needed to figure out how to work out the other areas of my life. How could I be fulfilled in other areas than just my businesses?
>
> It took a lot of time. I took a lot of courses. I did a lot of self-development, if that's what you want to call it. I had to take the time off and I had to change my environment, as well, because my identity was so caught up in the environment and people I was surrounded by. It was very hard for me to get out of that and get to the point I'm at today, but now I feel free again; I don't feel like I'm in a prison anymore.
>
> I started to put up new goals for myself in other areas beyond business, but it turned out I was just applying my old business discipline to the broader areas of my life. For instance, I'd have to take my new girlfriend out every Wednesday, like clockwork. I'd have to run 10 kilometers every day, eat this amount, drink this much water and take that amount of alkalizing greens.
>
> I soon realized there is no need to have a goal about everything. Life is a journey. The good thing is I'm much more conscious about it. I know how to get more harmony, and I know how to get more balance. Of course I get caught up and can get a one-directional, goal-setting mindset at times, but I now recognize the consequences. Now I know how to work with it. Now, I ask the question why-why-why am I doing this? Not just what am I doing?
>
> People have to see the compelling future that comes with making changes. I wouldn't have my daughter Isabella now if I hadn't made that choice. I wouldn't have this relationship where I feel so secure when I see my girlfriend. I just light up! I didn't have that in business. Here I have it every single moment. I have the joy of success, and not just in one way. This is so much more. That's what people have to step out of themselves and see. I chased all these goals business-wise and in education, but what I really wanted is this joy. Everybody wants to have that joy of life.

Like Markus, most of us have no idea what we're missing, which is why it's so easy to stay the course and skip the pit stop altogether. We don't get a peek into the other side of fulfillment without first letting go of our current course, and it's the requirement to let go with no promise of what's on the other side that keeps most in the fast-lane tailspin.

You may not be in a position to sell a business, stop production and move to Spain as Markus did, but perhaps you can relate to Phillip from chapter 5. He secretly stepped out of a top-tier university program to figure out his next steps:

> **MY ENERGY TOWARD** learning wasn't there. I didn't have that motivation, and I knew that if I were to stay at school that quarter, I would not have done well because my mind was so focused on healing myself that I needed to stop. I needed to refocus on the fundamentals in life.
>
> The reality is a lot of us grew up in an environment where we believe that stopping is not an option. Imagine if I were to go home and tell my mom, 'Yeah mom, I dropped out from school for a quarter so I can, to put it into cliché terms, 'find myself.'
>
> I didn't go to Europe or anything like that because I certainly didn't have the money. I stayed across town and worked through that time period, but that timeout was a means for me to identify the things that were important to me and really get in touch with my own spirituality.

The pit stop for Phillip meant stopping school completely. For you, it could mean stopping the overwhelming number of extracurricular activities you participate in—board meetings, PTA, sorority or fraternity committees—to free some time to be perfectly still. That might require streamlining your kids' activities so you're not pulled in so many different directions on the weekends. It might mean taking a total immersion personal growth retreat or even investing in a personal coaching program to get perspective on the design and strategies for the next phase of your life.

Whatever your method, owe it to yourself to do whatever it takes to get the physical time and mental space to dig deep and discover what true fulfillment looks like for you. If you're in the fast lane going in the wrong direction now, don't fool yourself into thinking your pit stop is just a weekend off. You took a long time to reach this place in your life, and it will take focused commitment to slowing down in order to change directions.

That doesn't mean you have to abruptly quit your job, as I did, because that is unrealistic for most. It does mean that you commit yourself to winning back the time to more consistently focus on you. It's crucial not only for your own sanity, but for the health of your marriage, your relationship with your kids and all the other areas of supreme importance to you.

As you're instructed before every airplane takeoff, in the event of an emergency, you must put your own mask on first before assisting a child (or anyone else). If you're in the wrong direction right now, make no mistake about it, this is an emergency.

So what do you actually do in the pit stop? What should you expect? The next section doesn't sound very appealing, but the truth is following this advice may be the most liberating experience you ever have:

1.) Stand Alone in the Dark With Your Fears

Sometimes our fears are so overwhelming that the "False Evidence Appearing Real" definition of fear just doesn't cut it. This is more than just the fear of failing, of going broke or losing your home. No, this is about what that fear means to you and what potentially negative beliefs reinforces what you may hold at your core.

"I think the fear I had to confront, find a way to resolve, and take the power back from is financial fear," Sophia said. "To put it simply, I'm afraid of running out of money. To me, that's very real. I've made decisions I felt weren't exactly what I wanted to do at the time, but the option would pay me better or the immediate return for the decision was more lucrative.

"In order to stand alone in the dark and try to figure out how to take some of the power back from that fear of insolvency, I had to try to understand what having money allowed me to do. Like, why was having money so important? And at the end of the day, having money for me was important:

1.) Because I have a strong need to be self-sufficient;
2.) I have a strong need to treat myself well, and…
3.) I don't trust there will be anybody else willing or able to take care of me.

"Not feeling like there's ever going be anybody who is able and willing to take care of me… that's a serious one that I still struggle with because at the heart of that is a fear of loneliness. I have a fear that I will go through the rest of my life being fundamentally unconnected and disconnected. I believe what the Bible says, 'It is not good for man or woman to be alone,' and I struggle to find ways to connect to myself. And so for me, a way to take some power back from that fear is through saving.

"So I need to have an extra amount of dollars just for savings and some sort of investment at all times because that represents something that will take care of me in the event that I'm unable. And I think it's important for individual people to figure out their fear, to say it out loud, to acknowledge it. Then once you say it out loud and acknowledge it, and you recognize how much power it has, then you can figure out what it will take to get that power back."

As daunting as standing alone in the dark with your fear may seem at the onset, it is crucial because, unbeknownst to you, those unspoken fears are driving every unproductive decision you are making in your life right now—guaranteed. This level of self-discovery can only take place in the pit stop, when you have quieted the noise and distractions, and made a decision to bravely acknowledge what shows up instead of sugarcoating it.

2.) Ask Different Questions

The second thing you must do in the pit stop is ask different questions—of yourself and other people. There's a cognitive psychology tool called the Johari Window. It is used to help people understand their interpersonal communication and relationships:

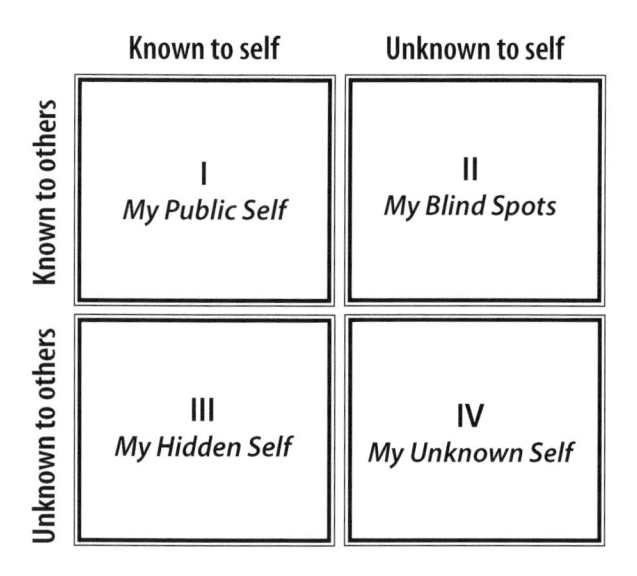

	Known to self	Unknown to self
Known to others	I My Public Self	II My Blind Spots
Unknown to others	III My Hidden Self	IV My Unknown Self

As you can see from the above diagram, your Public Self is what you allow people to know about you. For most of us, that Public Self includes the "presentable" parts of our lives—our achievements, our dreams and the cleaned-up version of who we are. When we are in the fast lane going in the wrong direction, we'll rarely find solutions on how to change by looking to the façade of our Public Self.

Your Blind Spots are the truths that are evident to other people but not so much to you. The Blind Spots are usually the very things that are keeping you from finding right direction in your life, whether that is your career, business, love life, health or whatever.

Your Hidden Self is what you purposely keep from other people. It's the yucky stuff—hidden challenges, pain and insecurities. The Hidden Self can also be the dreams and desires we refuse to acknowledge for fear of how others will react or for fear we won't be able to attain them.

Your Unknown Self is essentially the elements of your life that you and everyone around you are clueless about. I like to think of this as stuff only God knows, and it requires personal, spiritual and emotional growth to tap into the well of wisdom that is your Unknown Self.

What's really cool is as you reveal more of your Hidden Self, uncover your Blind Spots and ask deeper questions, you get to the root of what feels unknown and your whole world begins to open.

How do you do this?

Whatever questions you ask, your brain will find an answer. The problem is most of us are simply asking the wrong questions. So here's how you can use the Johari Window concept while you're in the pit stop:

When it comes to your Public Self, the question is easy. Ask yourself, "Is who I'm portraying myself to be in my career, in my business or in my relationships with family and friends really the true me? Or am I, as they say, 'faking the funk?'"

The true answer will come to you almost instantly. It might be a silent realization or a sensation somewhere in your body that confirms the truth. If the answer is negative in any way, your brain will immediately try to find every shred of evidence from your life to overturn that initial verdict. Don't mind your mind. It's simply trying to do its job, which is to protect you from pain and, in this case, the perceived pain comes with being honest about who you really are. For now, simply acknowledge the truth and try your best not to judge yourself for it.

When it comes to issues of your Hidden Self (the stuff you don't want other people to see), the common questions are: "How can I get over this? How can I hide this? How can I avoid this?"

You'll certainly get answers to those questions, but those answers won't get you any closer to your happiness, and your pit stop will be a waste of time. Instead, begin to ask yourself, "Who can help me with this? Whom can I trust with this? Who seems to have overcome this? Who might relate to me?"

Ask those types of questions and watch the floodgates of resources rush to your aid in acquiring what you want. You cannot move from wrong direction to right direction alone—it simply does not work like that. And, as you reveal more of your Hidden Self to other people who can help you, you'll find you have everything you need to truly live your life by design.

Our Blind Spots exist because, well, we are blind to them. And we remain blind to them because most of us don't value external input into our lives. Notice I said external input, not external validation. No one can validate you as being enough, yet other people's input can help you get over hurdles faster than you can on your own. That input can come from friends and family, from coaches and mentors or from your peers.

The most effective way to uncover your blind spots is to proactively seek input in your

> ## Conversations in the Fast Lane
>
> ✓ The hardest part about taking a pit stop is finding the time. Do you believe you have the time or do you feel completely overwhelmed by the demands on your life?
>
> ✓ If you're due (or overdue) for a pit stop, what can you rearrange in your life right now to create time and space for it?
>
> ✓ Tip: Take a written inventory of the activities and responsibilities that consume your time on a regular basis.
>
> ✓ Ask some close friends to objectively dissect how you are spending your time and provide honest feedback.
>
> ✓ Ask your friends for ideas on what you can batch, what you can delegate or outsource and how you can do some things more efficiently (especially with kids and family) to carve out some personal time. The amount of time may start out small, but when used consistently, your pit stop opportunities will grow.

life on a regular basis. When it comes to your business, your plans, your relationships, your endeavors, begin to ask:

- Am I viewing this situation the right way?
- How do you think I am handling this situation?
- What could I do differently?
- What should I consider that I'm not considering?
- What am I not seeing here?
- Do you notice a pattern in my behavior, actions, etc.?
- Is there something you see here that I'm not seeing?
- Am I approaching this the right way?
- What should I do next?
- What would you have done differently?

The point is to be teachable and coachable in our relationships. We often tell people stuff about our lives without inquiring of people about our lives. As a result, there are times when others see things in our character or our situations that we completely miss. They are unwilling to share their perspectives because we don't open ourselves to receive input and proactively seek these viewpoints.

Consequently, we end up going around in circles in our lives, suffering far longer than we should. In your pit stop, you want to ask more questions of other people to get insights into your life circumstances. You might be surprised at the answers that were right in front of you that you simply could not see.

Additionally, begin asking more questions of the areas of your life you feel are unknown. It is my belief that when there are nagging questions in your spirit, it's a summoning for you to go below the surface to get the answers. One technique that I find very useful for myself is what I call "Nested Questions." When you are trying to find answers and you ask the proverbial question, "Why?" the first answer that comes to mind is rarely the true answer. In fact, the second answer that comes to mind is rarely the true answer. You often must ask a deeper question of "Why?" to yourself four or five times to get to the authentic root.

For example, let's say you are a perfectionist to a fault. Your need for perfection keeps you working far more than you should and sucks the life out of you. For years, you have not been able to achieve balance in the other areas that are important to you.

So, ask yourself, "Why do I feel the need to be perfect?"

Because I don't want to make a mistake.

"Why am I afraid to make a mistake?"

Because people will know I don't know what I'm doing.

"Why am I afraid if people know that I don't know what I'm doing?"

Because they'll figure out I really don't belong here.

Bingo! That's the root issue. Most people stop at the first answer because it sounds reasonable; to go deeper takes too much time and too much honesty. But unless you go deeper, you'll never gain the freedom you really want. In the above example, if the person really believed they belonged in their role, they wouldn't feel the need to be perfect. In fact, they would welcome the growth that comes from other people's correction and input.

A pit stop is not a one-time occurrence. If you are committed to living your life to the absolute fullest, you'll see the pit stop as a gift and an opportunity to periodically check in with your life and ensure you are living it by your own design.

The reason most of us can't follow our heart
is we don't know what our heart really wants.
And we don't know what our heart wants because we
don't shut up long enough to listen.
We often spend so much time questioning whether
we measure up, what we should want and if it's
possible that we miss that very still voice that says,
"This is the way. Walk in it."
It is spot on every time.

CHAPTER 14
••••
Listen to Your Life

OPRAH WINFREY ONCE said, "As you become more clear about who you really are, you'll be better able to decide what is best for you—the first time around." I like to think that's true in all cases, but if we are honest with ourselves, we know it's not. I've rushed into many situations, fully aware that I was headed toward a train wreck. But I rationalized that somehow this time would be different—I wasn't like everybody else—and this would only be a temporary situation. The decision would justify itself.

I completely ignored all the warning signs and refused to listen to my life, and I got spanked for it every time. In my defense, in my earlier years, I didn't give much credence to those inner promptings. I was raised to use my head, not my heart or my intuition or any of those other "woo-woo" inner compasses.

Even when my head whispered, "Wrong direction," I held hard and fast when I made a decision. I would go down with the ship before bailing on my commitment, no matter how much pain I endured. I was no quitter, but when it came to discerning right direction for my life, I was deaf, blind and a little slow to get it.

It Is What It Is

A colleague's college-bound son was weighing his career options, and journalism was at the top of his list. She told him, "Journalists don't make a ton of money, but it could be a fascinating life." While there are a few exceptions, such as management, network on-air talent and high-profile columnists, the majority of journalists will generally agree their industry pays terribly, especially in the early years.

It is what it is.

What often creates discontentment is that we fail to see people and situations as they *are*, and then complain as if the circumstances should be different. We don't see our businesses as they are. We don't see our workplaces and relationships as they are, and we don't own the price tag associated with our choices.

If you choose to be a journalist, unless you become one of the exceptions, the fact you don't make a ton of money kinda just... is what it is. That doesn't mean you can't generate money in other ways, such as writing books or keynote speaking; it just means it might not come from your salary.

...*But it could be a fascinating life.*

If you want to be a preeminent figure in your industry *and* make six or seven figures from your company *and* you want to manage people *and* manage a family, all of that comes at a price. That price might be long working hours in which you miss the magical moments with your kids. It might mean challenging co-workers, brutal travel, crazy politics and vacations scheduled around fiscal year-ends, but it is what it is.

If you want greater stability and defined working hours, you might opt for a government career. You will deal with some sizable hair-raising bureaucracy and other experiences that, quite frankly, don't always make a lot of sense.

It is what it is.

If you want greater freedom, flexibility and control over your own time, then you may consider entrepreneurship, and that, too, comes at a price. That price might be a lot of risk, uncertainty, fear and challenges. It means putting yourself on a ledge and wondering if you'll emerge as a champ or a chump. It means making money and losing money and figuring out how to make money again. It's never a dull moment and rarely a "safe" one, at least in the beginning.

It is what it is.

Most people treat their work like a buffet line, where they request the most delectable of dishes and discard life's "Brussels sprouts." They want narrowly defined working hours with long-term job security. They want the freedom to come and go as they please with extended vacations and a mid-level executive's salary.

Sorry, dude, it doesn't work like that. It doesn't work like that in your career. It especially doesn't work like that with your marriage, and it most definitely doesn't work like that with your kids.

As soon as you recognize what *is,* and stop fighting what *is,* you can determine whether you really want what *is.* Your decisions will become easier because you can honestly embrace the trade-offs associated with your choices—in work, in love, in life—as opposed to denying that trade-offs exist. The drawback to acknowledging "what is," however, is that you're now fully accountable for the choices you make. No excuses, no shifting of blame.

So, with your hand on heart, when you look at the life you have created, is it what you *really* want?

If the answer is "no" for whatever reason, don't argue with yourself; it's settled. No wrestling, no rationalizing. Something needs to change and you must commit to figuring out how to make that change. I don't mean *if* you're going to change it; I mean *how* you're going to change it. End of discussion.

If the answer is "yes," ask yourself why. Sometimes we want things because everybody else seems to want them, as well. Do you know how many people have children simply because they think they should? Other people want something because they have something to prove.

A friend's father is a former prime minister to Barbados, has served as an ambassador to China and has been knighted by Queen Elizabeth. Growing up, my friend felt as if he had to contend with his father's legacy. So, yes, he wanted success, but the motivation was to surmount his dad. When what you want is rooted in your desire to prove that you're enough or better than the next person, you may as well hit the kill switch on that goal. *You will never be satisfied.*

If you're unclear about why you want what you want, then go back to the last chapter on the "Pit Stop" and apply the strategy for how to ask questions of yourself to get a true answer to this question. It might reveal more to you than you realize.

For Genevieve, that question led to a major, uncomfortable, but liberating change for her.

> "AT SOME POINT in my evaluation, I was asked if I wanted to be partner. I said, 'No.' So at that point, I sabotaged myself. People liked me, but I was considered not to be 'all-in' at the firm. That's a vulnerable thing. I didn't want to let it be known that I messed it up for myself."

Genevieve eventually left her law firm and set out on her own. It would be a fairy tale to report she lived happily ever after with her decision. The truth is, she is happier and healthier, but remember, there are trade-offs. For more freedom and flexibility, she's navigating through the newness of doing something completely unconventional. It's scary and lonely at times, but it will eventually pay off for what she wants. For Genevieve, this huge change meant she risked possible failure, but she had to listen to her life. Failing to do so would result in certain misery.

Most of us don't listen to our lives—the whispers or the screams. We don't listen when it comes to work. We don't listen when it comes to love. We don't listen when it comes to anything. Kathleen confirms:

"I lived in Puerto Rico at the time, but I always hated Puerto Rico, and I always wanted to leave," she said. "Then I ended up meeting and marrying a Puerto Rican man who always said that he would never leave. So that's a great example of being totally uncon-

> ### Conversations in the Fast Lane
>
> ✓ Have you acknowledged "what is" in your career, business or personal life, or are you playing ignorant to the truth of what's showing up?
>
> ✓ When you look at the life you have created, is it what you want?
>
> ✓ If the above answer is yes, why do you want the life you have? What are the motivating factors?
>
> ✓ If the answer is no, what exactly do you want? Don't worry at this stage if you don't know how to get it.
>
> ✓ Are there any perceived trade-offs to getting what you want right now?

- - -

scious and not thinking things through. Like, 'Okay, what's the plan here? You want to get out of Puerto Rico but you're marrying a man who never wants to leave?' So it was doomed to fail from the start. I tried hard to make the relationship work—really, really hard—and the harder I tried, the worse it got.

"It's the same principle when I was in the corporate world as it was when I was married to my ex-husband. I don't know if it's your higher voice, your higher power, your higher self, I don't know, but you do get these 'glimpses' sometimes. It's like a voice is saying, 'Get out of here, what are you doing here?'"

So, listening to your life isn't just about work, and it's definitely not about leaving a job. Please don't miss the point. It's about listening to what your life is telling you *about you* and making the necessary decisions to heed that message, even if those decisions scare the wits out of you.

If you fail to listen in one area of your life, nine times out of 10 you play ignorant in all the others, and you're paying a price for it. You may excuse your circumstances by saying you're confused, that you don't know what to do or what you want. I believe you know exactly what you want. You may not know how to get what you want, you may be afraid of the risk(s) to get it, but you know exactly what you want.

Kill the noise, limit the input from well-meaning friends and simply listen to your life. It's the best advice you will ever receive.

Every now and then in life, you have to go
on strike, complete with picket signs,
and chants of, "Hell no, we won't go!"
Only when you demand more from life will you
experience more money, more benefits,
more laughter, more joy, vitality, energy and love.
Everything—*absolutely everything*—is negotiable.

CHAPTER 15
····
Stand Up For Your Life

SOMETIMES YOU GET pushed to take a stand for your life when your spirit gives you an answer you don't want to admit is true. That's exactly what happened to me when my first business partnership disintegrated.

At one point, I thought I could never accomplish my dreams without my partner. By the end, I knew I would never accomplish my dreams with her. In fact, I would become a very bitter, broken person if I didn't do something. I had to listen to my life and take a stand, whether I wanted to or not.

Taking a stand goes far beyond your occupation. If you truly desire to be free, you will have to take a stand in your relationships, partnerships, activities and even (or especially) with your family. What does taking a stand really look like and how do you accomplish it?

By deliberately making decisions in line with what you want, and only what you want.

Most of us make decisions to assuage our fears, which is generally the opposite of what we want. I made the decision to stay in the business partnership 18 months longer than I should have because I was afraid I couldn't hack it on my own. I wanted nothing more than to be free of the drama, yet I was too scared to take a stand.

When you envision how you want your family life to be, the time you want to spend and the richness you want to experience, then it's your responsibility to make choices in your career, business and with how you use time management to support that vision. Of course, there are moments when you have to deviate from what you want by necessity, but those are "for now" choices, not forever ones.

You must be very clear with yourself that making those choices is a means to a very specific end.

Unconventional Choices

Taking a stand invariably requires you to make some unconventional choices. My friend Regina is a senior executive with a large telecommunications company. She and her husband were featured in *Essence* magazine for their choice to put family first at the expense of modern mindsets. Regina shared:

> "OUR PLAN WAS to have these dynamic careers and be gangbusters for the rest of our lives!" she said. "We also planned to have three children and so much more. I don't know how we would have fit it all in, so it's no surprise God had a totally different plan for us.
>
> Our plan was never to have my husband be a stay-at-home dad to our one son, but I have no idea how I would do the job I do today—and we would certainly not have the family life we have—without my husband being at home. When we decided to go this route for our family, there were absolute challenges, and many of them were external because of the appearance and shift in our whole family dynamic.
>
> It was a shift for my husband because we were investing in his career at the time. He had attended business school in Chicago, and I was going to sit back and relax a bit. While my career was going well, he realized that Corporate America really wasn't for him. So we decided the best option for our family was for him to stay home with our son.
>
> I give him an awful lot of credit because I don't think there are many men as intelligent and strong in character as he is that could take the position at home. The one thing we did—and continue to do every day—is reinforce that my husband is the man of the house. Especially since we have a son, it's important that he respects the roles that his parents have in the household. It all works together because we are committed to the roles as husband and wife—as father and mother in the relationship, and because he is so supportive of my career and me. That's why it works beautifully. I get to do what I do outside of the home and come back in the home and be the wife. I like the security of our marriage as equally as I like security of my career."

Regina remembers the time and place when her husband called himself a stay-at-home dad. They had people over for dinner, and there's always that question of "What do you do?"

"Typically, it's, 'I work for this company or my business is this or my background is that,' " she recalled. "But, he said, 'I am a stay-at-home dad.' We had never really talked about that, but I can remember the peace he had on his face when he said it. And for me to know that he had claimed something he could embrace, that he was at peace and was firm, gave me so much relief."

When you know who you are and what you really want, you make decisions to get what you want instead of decisions that merely make you look as if you have what you want. What we can learn from Regina's story is getting to the "right direction" in our lives sometimes requires us to make decisions that seem contrary to what most people would ever conceive.

Going from the corporate gangbuster couple to their current family dynamic is not what Regina's friends or family would have envisioned. But corporate gangbusting was a means to an end, to the security and stability of all members of their family, including their son. When that means no longer accomplished the desired end, it was time for a Plan B.

There will always come a time when your Plan A no longer works, whether that's in your business, with your kids, even with your personal health. In those moments, will you, like Regina and her husband, have the courage to set a new standard and make unconventional choices? Will you be willing to make decisions that get you what you really want instead of decisions that merely make you look as if you have what you want?

Tough Conversations

Standing up for your life will clearly have a profound impact on you personally, but you might be rocking the lifeboat for a lot of other people, as well. Most people are really afraid to confront that reality. It could range from breaking off a relationship that no longer works to changing the dynamic in a friendship that's holding you back. For Nick, it was explaining to his family how his career decisions would affect them:

"We all get to a point where we're like, 'Why am I doing this? Why am I living my life for others?'" he said. "They are important others, don't get me wrong, but at what point do you say, 'I'm going to live the life that I want to live,' as opposed to, 'I'm going to live the life that makes everybody else able to live the life they want to live?' And that's what I was doing. I was basically living my life to make sure that my parents and family lived the lives they wanted in a comfortable setting.

"So, I had a heart-to-heart conversation with them. I told them I would have to stop supporting particular efforts because I was going to make a career shift of my own. They had to come to terms with the fact that I wouldn't be subsidizing a lot of stuff, and that was scary to them because I had been doing it for 10 years.

"Once we figured out how the shift was going to happen, then it was just a progression of baby steps. I cut down my hours at work and eventually left altogether. I started taking on contract gigs and giving my family the tools to do the financial planning they needed to do since the income would no longer be coming from me. I basically reversed the situation by having them understand the changes I was going through and how those changes would affect them in return. They were actually more supportive than I thought they'd be."

As Nick's story illustrates, often our fear of a tough conversation is worse than the conversation itself. People who love you will still love you, and they'll commit to working through the transition, no matter how convoluted or painful the situation might be. For those who don't love you enough to be there for you, learn to put on your "big boy" pants and keep it moving.

Setting Boundaries

The hardest thing to do when taking a stand for your life is to set new boundaries. Abigail is a former management consultant and senior director for a high-end hotel chain. You may be very challenged by her story if you have been in the professional world for some years with limited personal boundaries.

Abigail: I credit my current boundaries to being in management consulting. In my third year, I got burned out because I was working seven days a week. The straw that broke the camel's back was when we were working on a project proposal. I came in on Sunday at noon and didn't finish until 3 p.m. the next day. Colleagues were coming in on Monday, and I was in shorts and flip-flops from the weekend. I had been up for more than 24 hours and was getting ready to leave when someone was like, "Hey, I need to pull you into this proposal. Can you come in and do this?" I couldn't believe it. I was tired, bloodshot, and they still wanted more.

I provided them with what they needed, then went home and curled up in a ball crying. I talked to my mom, and she said, "You've had enough," and I agreed. I called HR and asked how long I could be gone and still have a job. Within two weeks, I took a leave of absence. I left in early November and didn't return until January. After that point, I never again made work disproportionately more valuable to my happiness than anything else in my life.

I learned that lesson early, and I don't measure my success or fast lane status by anybody else's definition. I'm comfortable doing good work, and I will do good work between the hours of 7:30 a.m. and 6 p.m., with occasional late nights. I will be done by 5 p.m. on Friday and you will not hear from me or receive an email from me until Monday. That is my time, and I am uncompromising.

Me: How did you ever implement those boundaries and get other people to respect them?

Abigail: When I came back from leave, I met with my boss to ask for an adjusted work schedule—four 10-hour days with Friday as a flex day. So, I made a documented change in my personnel file, which didn't last very long due to the nature of the business. I also asked my boss' advice of people she thought had good work/life balance, and I had a conversation with one guy whose principles I adopted into my own life. He said:

1.) Figure out what's incredibly important to you and don't compromise on that.

For him, it was incredibly important to walk his children to the bus in the morning. So, he would not get to the office before 9:15 and wouldn't accept a meeting before 9:30. Sure, that could be inconvenient for a client who wants to meet at 8, but it was important for him to eat breakfast with his daughters and take them to school in the morning, so he would not compromise.

2.) Be so good at what you do that people will deal with your boundaries.

3.) Be very clear about what you want to do and can do instead of focusing on the things that you're not good at doing. Find a way to have others help you do those things. Play to your strengths and work smarter. His personal example was that he was incredibly strong technically, but wasn't a good client schmoozer. So, he sent more junior people on the team to the networking events, which they loved, and spent his time on the analytics. He could zip through the technical in less time, and it was less energy draining.

So I took that advice and set my boundaries. When I came back from leave, emails were flying on a Friday afternoon. One read, "Hey, I was hoping to incorporate your feedback and get this out on Monday." The request obviously assumed I'd be willing to work over the weekend. My response was, "Got it—not able to work this weekend. I'll come in early on Monday at 6:30 a.m. if you need me, but I'm not working on this before Monday."

I do not give up my personal time. I don't get paid enough. Whether I'm a manager or a senior vice president doesn't mean that I owe you more time. The company has not bought more of my time, in my opinion, so I stick to that.

Me: Many people would consider their fast-paced environment and wonder how the heck they can take a stand in their life? You were in your 20s and fairly junior within the organization at the time. Did you get pushback from people when you announced these were your boundaries?

Abigail: In all honesty, with certain exceptions, I would say no, mainly for a couple of reasons. One, when I left and took a leave of absence, I was already seen as top talent, so they were willing to accommodate me without losing me. I knew I had some leverage. They asked me, "What can we do to help you feel more balanced?"

So, I proposed the things I wanted to initially start doing, and I had immediate support because my leaders knew why I had taken leave in the first place. There was interest on their part to not let me burn out again. When months went by and people forgot about the "arrangement," I still stayed true to those boundaries. The organization will test you to see how steadfast you are to those boundaries, and I held fast.

Me: What did your career trajectory look like from that point on?

Abigail: The next year, I was promoted, and the following year I was promoted again. It actually helped me because I think when you're working long hours and you're working a lot, sometimes you can be doing more but not to any greater ends than if you were doing less. I was able to laser focus, so I could say, "No, I'm not working on that proposal," or "Don't staff me on that project. I've spoken to my manager and here's the next experience I want to have." I was able to be clearer and not just be busy doing work for work's sake. I was working smart.

If you're good at what you do and you have established yourself, people will give you some level of latitude. I don't look at other people to measure how good I am. I'm okay with the results that come with that, because I'm not willing to compromise on how to get there. I may be slower on my path because I work eight- or nine-hour days and don't work on weekends. I thank God for the consulting experience because it very early gave me these lessons that 40-year-olds are learning now. I won't make those mistakes now because I made them very early.

Me: Do you think you lost any ground on your career trajectory by having those boundaries?

Abigail: I personally don't think so. I look at my peer group, and I think I'm tracking on par with where they're at and what they're earning. In fact, I might be ahead of some of them, even the ones who have MBAs, which I don't.

Me: What advice would you give others considering similar moves toward greater balance?

Abigail: You're going to put in some hard time, but you must do it to a clear end. I had that breakdown in consulting, but I had worked up to that point to be seen as a valuable and key player. If you're doing that kind of work to establish yourself as credible, do it with a clear end—that the company will value you enough to put up with your boundaries in due time. But you have to be good at what you do. If you're setting eight-hour boundaries and what you're producing in that time is crap, it's not going to work. You have to produce.

Abigail's strategies and perspectives are so valuable and in line with the core principles I use with my coaching members. We have to be very, very proactive about how we strategically design our lives because in the fast lane it's easy to get caught up in activity for the sake of activity. And we all know that activity does not always lead to results, nor does it lead to happiness.

Abigail was young in her career when the breakdown happened that transformed her perspective on work/life balance. The decisions she made regarding how much time she invested and which projects she accepted created a path of least resistance for her, and she avoided the land mine that could have been more physically, spiritually and emotionally draining over time.

Abigail paid her dues before making demands on her employer. She had already demonstrated that she was "keeper" talent, and you'll have to do the same. Where most

> ## Conversations in the Fast Lane
>
> ✓ Are you being pushed to take a stand in some area of your life? If so, what's stopping you?
>
> ✓ What tough conversations do you need to have with people in order to take a stand for yourself?
>
> ✓ Are you working to earn the right to set more boundaries in your life, or are you working to earn the right to work even more?
>
> ✓ How do you feel knowing that nobody owes you anything and the quality of your life and how you manage it is your responsibility?
>
> ✓ What can you do to set boundaries to reclaim more time or have more balance? What are the "ifs, ands, and buts" excuses that prevent you from setting those boundaries?

fast-laners go wrong, however, is they don't leverage their value to the company in a way that benefits them. They continue to give and give and give, hoping superiors or customers will notice their efforts and somehow reward them. They'll reward your efforts, all right, and if you don't advocate for yourself, your diligence will be rewarded with more work and added responsibility without any increase in personal fulfillment.

Find Your Truth

This might offend you, but if you believe your company or kids or place of worship owes you something for your sacrifices, you are completely wrong. In actuality, the company has no responsibility other than paying you in accordance with their contractual obligation. Your kids don't owe you squat. The charities and the boards you sit on do not owe you anything. Your quality of life and how you manage it is your responsibility. The company will take whatever it can, your boards will take whatever they can and your kids will take whatever they can… and they will have the nerve to ask for even more.

Believe me, if you drop dead tomorrow, your customers will find another service provider and the company will find somebody else to take your place. Your stuff won't even be cleared out of your desk before the next person is sitting in it, with or without the ghost of your greatness.

So ask yourself what all your hustle and bustle is really about. Moreover, is it worth it? For me, I realize everything I do now is for freedom—financial freedom, time freedom, freedom to love and experience life without being bogged down with "things."

That's my truth. It doesn't have to be yours, but I implore you to find your own.

Forgive fast. Forgive often.
Not for "them," but for you.

CHAPTER 16
• • • •
Forgiveness

OKAY, SO WHAT does forgiveness have to do with the fast lane or the wrong direction? Everything.

Throughout this book are myriad examples of people who found themselves in the fast lane going in the wrong direction. Those examples show that our detours are often rooted in something that someone did to us, said to us or how they made us feel. It may have been that parent who conditioned us to never accept failure; now we desperately run away from it. It may have been that well-intentioned mentor who taught us all about no pain/no gain; so we suffer in situations when all signs say to cut our losses. It may have been a bully who pushed us around; now we must prove we can't be beat. It may have been a father's standards we could never live up to; so we're chasing any achievement that will put us one up over him. It could have even been the cheating lover who left us penniless, forcing us to step up and find our strength; now, our success is an impenetrable fortress around our heart.

The roots vary, but the result is the same. We end up *screwed!*

If you find yourself still struggling in a particular area of your life, there may be some forgiveness that needs to happen—forgiveness of other people and, most of all, forgiveness of yourself. Until you are able to bless the very situations that caused you pain—abuse, bad advice, poor choices, your need for validation, your lack of self-esteem—you will never, ever fully be free.

Translation: You'll make the same mistakes over and over again. It might be a different game with different players, but you'll have the same outcome. So you have two choices: forgive or relive.

Where there is no forgiveness for another person, you remain a victim to that person.

Whether you realize it or not, they control you. Where there is no forgiveness for yourself, you'll be plagued with a shame that no amount of achievement can cure. I love this quote:

> **No man is your enemy, no man is your friend; every man is your teacher.**
> — Author unknown

I soooo wish I could give proper credit to the originator because this quote altered my perspective on a busted business partnership. Truth be told, that partner was the absolute best teacher I've ever had. As painful as the partnership was, I would not be the person I am today without that experience, so I guess I have her to… *uh*… thank.

And I do.

Ultimately, you're responsible for the decisions you have made, regardless of how other people may have contributed to those decisions. Until you choose to bless those "teachers" in your life, no matter how horrible you perceive their lessons were to you, you cannot unlock the seeds of blessing that their role has planted in your life. For instance, a spouse who cheated holds the seeds to the qualities of the man or woman you may love for the rest of your life the next time around.

One of my coaching members, Rachel, is a dynamic tech professional for a telecommunications company in South Africa. When she first approached me about coaching, she had three main objectives:

- To gain clarity on her dreams and goals, and determine a plan for attaining them;
- To break through the ceiling she had reached in her life and career and open up her potential to be passionate and motivated again;
- To get comfortable going after her goals solely for her own benefit, not anyone else's.

What's fascinating about Rachel's story is that the reason she came to me for guidance was not the *reason* she came to me. Not at all!

We must first understand Rachel's life and background. Both her parents died of AIDS when she was a teenager—first her mother, then her father. While her father was moderately well off financially, he did not leave a will distributing his estate. Rachel was one of several brothers and sisters, and her older sibling siphoned her father's money and left Rachel penniless to care for her baby sister. Rachel did what she had to do for survival and to ensure her sister received an education while her other siblings were of little support. Over time, Rachel worked hard to become very successful, but she also became very bitter.

When we began working together, Rachel had no idea how that bitterness had transformed who she was as a person. She had become guarded, hostile and cynical.

Her joy was gone and her dreams were stymied. During one of our calls, she shared that for the first time in over a decade, she had walked through the streets of an old neighborhood where she experienced unspeakable pain and abuse. She went from smoking 20 cigarettes a day to four in a matter of a couple of weeks. She put on a pretty dress and went dancing for the first time in ages. The kicker, however, was an email she sent to me some time later.

> Hi Renessa,
> I arrived from Zambia today exhausted. My Gran passed so I went for the funeral and spent two days with family. Wow! Let me tell you how much I've grown. Being around my family, who are all strong-headed, used to be so hard. I'd just run, angry each time.
> This time, I was fully present, watching people and listening. Yes actually listening… And the realisation again is that the tables have so turned. I'm definitely more in control of me. Not once did I lose my temper, not once did I disregard anyone or their opinion. The new me is just awesome! All the formed opinions on people within the extended family have been dispelled and now I just want to get to know people and let them tell their story. I'm praying everyday for forgiveness for my old ways and grateful everyday for my newfound peace. I'm so in love with the new me—gentle, kind, generous, thoughtful, honest to others and self. The list goes on.

Rachel, like most of us, thought the key to her progress would be in new goals and strategies for attaining them. She had no idea the unresolved issues with her family (and herself) were at the root of her diminishing passion. However, when Rachel realized the issue, she took full responsibility for the part she played in perpetuating the dysfunctional family dynamic—despite how she had been wronged. More importantly, she took responsibility for what needed to happen next.

So, at what point will you choose to take responsibility for your past hurts? Taking responsibility isn't just "getting over it" and hoping it no longer bothers you. Taking responsibility is actually finding the learning in the hurt, acknowledging any deficiencies in you that may have contributed to your offense and appreciating who you get to become as a result of that teaching. Rachel's email was all about the changes she was making within herself.

You may be reading this book and recounting unspeakable abuse from your childhood. I am in no way suggesting that you did anything to cause or deserve what happened. What I *am* saying is you must take responsibility for how you have consciously or unconsciously responded to those wrongs, and how you have allowed them to impact your life, even as your awareness grew. That is all on you.

With my business partner, as much as I resented how marginalized I felt at times in

> **Conversations in the Fast Lane**
>
> ✓ How has a lack of forgiveness impacted your ability to take your life to the next level or overcome a nagging struggle?
>
> ✓ Can you look back on people or situations that caused you tremendous pain and actually bless the seeds that were planted as a result?
>
> ✓ While you certainly may not have deserved past wrongs done to you, have you taken responsibility for how you responded to the hurt?
>
> ✓ Is there anyone you need to forgive, and is there anyone you need to forgive again?
>
> ✓ Is there a decision or disappointment that you need to forgive yourself for?

. . . .

that professional relationship, I was too insecure in my own abilities to take a stand. I *allowed* all that to happen.

The seed that was planted from that experience was an empowering self-assurance and trust in God to take my life to a completely new level. So, I can do nothing but bless my teacher. Forgiveness was not easy, and every now and then residual emotions surface, and I have to go through the process of forgiveness again. But I am committed to taking full responsibility and letting it go.

My business partner isn't the only one I had to forgive. When I recounted the years of frustration in that relationship, I couldn't believe I actually allowed it to happen. I couldn't believe I was so intimidated. I couldn't believe I questioned my abilities so much. I couldn't believe I compromised my own self-respect in some ways. While my feelings toward my partner created anger and resentment, I felt nothing but shame for myself.

I needed to forgive me.

I needed to forgive the young woman who didn't believe in herself, for eventually she taught me just how much I do bring to the marketplace. I needed to forgive the young woman who was afraid to speak her mind; she taught me to set boundaries without having to fight for them. That woman was an amazing teacher! She did the best she could with what she knew at the time, and when things got tough, she rose to the occasion and transformed into the equally amazing woman who gets to share these experiences with you now.

Forgiveness is essentially a pardon for an offense. The perpetrator owes you nothing more—no apology, no groveling, no recompense. They don't even have to *ask* for your forgiveness!

Gulp. Now hold on a minute.

Don't mistake what I am saying. To forgive does not suggest what the other person did was okay, nor does it mean the person is absolved from karma's swift kick in the pants. What it does mean is that you relinquish your demand to the universe that justice be rendered at your hand. It's a real and symbolic declaration that you need nothing more from your perpetrator to make you whole. You are completely free.

And when you are no longer enslaved by the emotions of people who hurt you or the ways you may have disappointed yourself, you make decisions from a place of freedom. You have nothing to prove, nothing to compensate for and no one to impress. You will choose clearly the right answer for *you* instead of choosing the answer that pleases the overly critical voice of some authority figure in your head. And, you will say, "No, thank you" to all choices that do not serve the life you are designing for yourself.

As ugly as the road to forgiveness can be emotionally, your life truly becomes your own when you master the art of forgiving—the big and small offenses. You will have plenty of unsolicited opportunities to practice.

When you deliberately decide
not to live your mission,
you experience an inner loathing,
for you know in your heart that you
have punked out of life.

CHAPTER 17

••••

What Is Your Passion For Now?

EVERYBODY HAS A "thing." You know, the "thing" that makes you tick. For some, it's all about family. For others, it is about finding the ideal career path. For me, it was about preeminence. I just wanted to be exceptionally good at something that made a difference for a lot of people. That's why I was so discontent in my previous careers. I was a high-performer on the job because I had a strong work ethic to achieve, but I wasn't naturally good at the jobs. I couldn't believe nobody else seemed to figure that out.

I always viewed myself as the "jack-of-all-trades-master-of-none" employee. That bothered me for some inexplicable reason. I didn't need to be better than someone else for the sake of ego; I simply desired to be uniquely exceptional at something. I resonate so deeply with Erma Bombeck's quote, "When I stand before God at the end of my life, I would hope that I would not have a single bit of talent unused and could say, 'I invested everything you gave me wisely.'"

The problem was I couldn't be preeminent at something I couldn't stand to do—and I was doing a lot of work that I couldn't stand doing.

You may think differently for yourself, and that's okay. Preeminence was my "thing." And when you are clear-minded on your thing, you can begin to understand the tradeoffs required to get it. To live my mission, I had to let go of security—job security, financial security, even the security of living life in a conventional way. I couldn't be safe *and* preeminent; they were mutually exclusive. Once I understood that, I began to make decisions very differently.

Added to preeminence for me is freedom, followed by love and connection. Of the three, freedom might actually be my number one value. It permeates how I view children, marriage, work, everything. At one time, I was all about security. Having grown up watching my parents struggle financially, every decision I made in college and my professional life was to build financial security, protect myself and provide for my needs.

That need for security created a tremendous amount of pain because it led to decisions that made me unhappy, even though they seemed right at the time. So, while the desire for security is not wrong in and of itself, I eventually realized valuing security above all else could not get me what I ultimately wanted in my life.

So, what do you value? Security? Image? Contribution? Love? Connection? Growth? Praise? Whatever you value will drive every decision you make. As you begin to get honest with yourself about what's missing in your life, you can determine whether your values are the culprits.

For instance, if one of your top values is your image and how other people perceive you, then you must ask yourself if having image as your top value in any way prevents you from getting other things you want, such as love and connection. Are there risks you shy away from because you're afraid of how it might tarnish your image if you fail? If you are chronically unfulfilled, I bet you'll discover that your highest values, your "thing," might be conflicting with what you truly want.

Your Passion For Now

Beyond the elusive concept of life purpose, I believe you're able to find what a friend calls your "passion for now" when you implement a lot of the principles discussed in this book. When you're able to be honest and open… to not worry that someone else's success is at your expense… to recognize the world is not one big competition… there will be room for you to explore whether the direction of your fulfillment today is the same or different from where you started years ago. When you get to the place where you are willing to do what it takes to change lanes, then you are primed to discover your passion for now, your life purpose or both.

My friend Joey and I were having a discussion about passion, and I was fascinated by what he shared:

"WHEN YOU START talking about being aligned with your passion, I think some people reading this book would be scared by that because they don't know what their passion is. They might get caught in a loop of 'I need to figure out my passion before I can do anything,' and that's a really dangerous place to be. I'm somewhat of a believer in 'What's my passion for now?'

Trying on different passions like you would try on different outfits is a good thing. It's the passion for the time. It's the willingness to be authentic, the willingness to say,

'I'm not exactly sure.' How many times do people in the fast lane say, 'You know, I'm not sure?' Sometimes we must get comfortable with the fact that we don't know the answer. If someone could get to the point where they say, 'I don't know what my life purpose is, but for now the thing I'm committed and focused on is this, this and this.' If, at the core, you're willing to be real and authentic, then the other stuff tends to sort itself out. "

Living your purpose can be an overwhelming concept for the very reasons Joey mentions. Most of us are very accustomed to having a well-laid plan for our life. As life gets more complicated with spouses, kids, mortgages, aging parents, busted economies and so forth, that plan takes on increasing importance. I am reminded of a quote attributed to multiple authors whenever I get overly attached to my plans:

"If you want to hear God laugh, tell him your plans."

That's certainly the truth when it comes to passion or life purpose or mission or destiny or whatever you want to call your plans. There are some lucky folks who come out of the womb with purpose written all over them. And then there are the rest of us.

There are two things you need to understand very clearly about purpose:

1.) Purpose Is Not Necessarily a Vocation

There are plenty of people who have no real zest for their work. They are content with their job, but their real passion is raising their kids, supporting a hobby or doing something altogether different. If that is you, own that passion as your life purpose, make decisions that support that purpose and stop trying to be something you are not. Your life purpose does not have to equate to a vocation.

Fellow Stanford graduate Delise is a stay-at-home mom. She was faced with these value decisions early in her college career and describes how they played out for her and her family:

" **FOR AS LONG** as I can remember, I wanted to be a physician. I decided to attend a physicians' panel to hear them discuss life in the medical field. 'I planned to have my first child in my third year of residency so that she/he would be too young to know I was never home,' said a female panelist. That statement hit me like a ton of bricks. I left thinking: 'It can't be that serious… can it?'

Over the next several weeks, I grappled with the thought of having to plan my pregnancies. I wondered how I would balance my home and work life. I contemplated whether I was willing to sacrifice family time for my career. Did I love medicine enough? I soon found myself in the office of my mentor, who happened to be a psychiatrist, (which was exactly what I needed in the middle of an identity crisis)! For the first time in my life, I expressed aloud that I did not want to be a doctor.

Now, I had no clue how to answer the, 'What do you want to be when you grow up?' question. The construction of my identity was completely tied to that career goal, and I couldn't seem to think outside that box. With my mentor's help and a newly active prayer life, I found my most genuine answer: 'I don't know, and I'm okay with that.'

From that point forward, I let go of my need to know, my need to plan, my need to understand. I graduated from Stanford with my Human Biology undergraduate degree and, a year later, with my Master's. I decided to move to Washington, D.C., without securing a job. There was freedom in letting go of my plans and just 'going with the flow!'

No amount of planning would have given me the opportunity to serve as an appointee in the Executive Office of the D.C. mayor, and since I was no longer wedded to positions and status, I also had no problem resigning from that position to help a California-based non-profit replicate their financial literacy programs in D.C. However, in a few short years, I would come full circle with my decision.

In March 2003, I ended a long-term relationship and decided to try something I've never done—join a gym. I remember looking around the weight room one evening, wondering if any of the men in there would turn out to be my husband. He could be anywhere, right? Him? *Nope.* Him? *Nope.* Him? *Nope.* Two years later, one of those "nopes" was exactly who I needed in my life, and we were married in April 2005. Turns out he likes to swim upstream, as well. Our motto: 'If everyone else is going left, we're going right.' And, he would never have married a doctor!

"So now, I am just enjoying things day-by-day. I don't need to know what happens at the end of the story. I am walking in faith that God's got that all under control. I'm focused on creating amazing memories for my family, starting with greeting my husband with a smile when he returns home from work and exploring the D.C. area (and beyond) with my children. From home-cooked meals to family vacations, from play dates and mommy groups to serving those in need, from homeschooling to cloth diapering, I am living the life that I could have never imagined. And each day is an adventure as a result."

Delise was courageous, even as a young woman. She didn't get caught up in the fact she had already earned degrees, that people had expectations of her becoming a doctor or being a doctor is what she had wanted to do most of her life. She was true to her "thing" (family) and she made choices—not knowing the outcome—to prioritize her thing.

Even now, Delise publishes a blog titled "Our Life Memories," which provides honest, useful reviews of family-friendly things to do in Washington, D.C. She and her family exude such joy! If ever there was a family I'd want to emulate, it would be hers. Family is her "passion for now" and that passion impacts more people than she realizes.

> ## Conversations in the Fast Lane
>
> ✓ Do you feel as if you are on your life purpose right now, or have you gotten swept up in the day-to-day?
>
> ✓ What's your "thing" that makes you tick and lights you up?
>
> ✓ Has the thought of finding your life purpose overwhelmed you? Is the concept of having a "passion for now" any easier to embrace?
>
> ✓ Have you ever confused life purpose with vocation?
>
> ✓ What is your "passion for now," and what can you do today to move that passion forward?

2.) Things Change

The second principle you should understand (and will likely protest) is that, yes, "things" change. And guess what? You get to change with them.

If you're on a quest for purpose, it's a safe bet your purpose will not be the first, second or even third thing you try—but you'll never find that purpose until you embark on the first, second or third idea. Sitting on the sidelines awaiting divine epiphany is a ticket to a life of potential with little fulfillment.

Over the years, I have had a lot of business ideas. For each venture, I would purchase a new Internet domain name in anticipation of my new project. At last count, I had about 16 different website domain names for past and future ventures. You could tell my direction based on the email domain I was using at the time. I had various real estate ventures, pursued network marketing, conducted women's seminars, you name it. I drove people crazy! I guess I was following my "passions for now." And through my first, second… fifth try, I uncovered what I believe to be my life purpose.

At least for now.

In fact, it was the passion for now that taught the lessons comprised in *Fast Lane, Wrong Direction*. My motivations for some of those past pursuits were wildly out of line with who I was and what I wanted. But the good news is I didn't allow ignorance of my ultimate purpose to stop me from moving ahead.

If you don't have the complete picture, that's okay. Avoid getting caught up in the perceived bigness of your "life's purpose." What you know today is enough to begin living your mission, your passion—for *now*.

The next step you should take is connected to the interests and options that are in front of you now. If you focus on what you *know* to do instead of what you *don't know* to do later, you will be amazed by how fast you'll progress. How counterintuitive is that?!

"I wasn't fully convinced that you could draw pictures and get paid to do so. Yet in my advertising business, that's essentially what I do."

— Joey, chief experience composer, *Design Symphony*

CHAPTER 18
••••
Intersection Between Passion and Marketplace

THE OBVIOUS QUESTION for all of us, whether we're about living our life purpose or just living our "passion for now," is, "How the heck do I get paid for this?" Understandably, this question doesn't apply if your passion is a hobby or a pastime you have no intention of ever making into a vocation.

Fast-laners generally want to hear more than just, "Do what you love and the money will come." We want to know the what, when, where and how. The frustration for fast-laners in the wrong direction is they know how to succeed… well, sort of.

Most have experienced some kind of professional success, they are well-respected and likely in some ways envied by people around them. But often they don't enjoy the thing they are "good" at doing and have no idea how to make the transition into successfully doing what they "enjoy." There is definitely a way to achieve this goal, but it's often a matter of whether or not you're up to the challenge.

Felix, a research analyst turned marketing director turned interior designer, shares:

"I know African-Americans are especially afraid of the arts. When I was in high school, I was always told to go for engineering, science and math. These are the things that will suit you well. These are the things that will prepare you and help you have a good life. I fed into that 110 percent, and I was miserable because it wasn't who I was.

"It wasn't indicative of what I wanted to do with my life, but it was what I thought would be good for me and good for my family in the long term. Let me say that I'm more than happy with where I'm at now because I think I'm being true to who I am and who I've always been."

Back in my engineering days, I was sold the same bill of goods as Felix about the benefits of "math, science and being black," and there truly were many benefits; they just weren't benefits that led to any level of enthusiasm or excitement for me. It took me a long time to be able to put the words "work" and "excitement" in the same sentence. Like Felix, I feel that I am now more true to who I am than ever before.

But how do you get there, at least with your line of work? How do you find the intersection between your passions and the marketplace? For over 10 years, the answer to that question completely eluded me, and through that old-fashioned school of hard knocks, I began to figure it out.

I once heard a speaker share three questions she asks of people who are trying to find that intersection between their passions and the marketplace:

- What are your passions?
- What are your strengths and skills?
- What does the marketplace want?

I don't know the speaker's context for the questions, but remembering them provided an interesting framework for this chapter as I share my own thoughts about how to apply those questions.

What Are Your Passions?

You must be truthful with yourself about your passions. You won't believe how challenging that truth is for some, or the myriad of lies people tell themselves to keep from owning up to what they truly want! Some worry what other people will think of their passion, especially if they've invested so much time and energy going down another path. Others question whether their passion has any real value in the marketplace. We can universally agree being a doctor saving lives is crucially important. Baking cupcakes? Not so much, right?

Not so.

At least not for The Learning Channel's "DC Cupcake" ladies, who have an entire television show dedicated to… *baking cupcakes*. It doesn't matter whether you value cupcake baking or not, some cable network valued their talent and innovation enough to give them their own show.

The point is, if you don't get honest about what you really want to do or be, you set yourself up to chase "false positives," pursuits that you've convinced yourself are your passions because they are "acceptable" pursuits. But they really don't satisfy you—and never will. I was so guilty of that!

Most of my entrepreneurial pursuits came about because of false positives. I convinced myself that providing quality housing options or helping people attain financial freedom through a home business was my passion, and I couldn't have been more disillusioned when I found the work so uninspiring. Those pursuits were dreadful chores for me, and I hated them. But I programmed myself to believe that the financial freedom I would enjoy when I succeeded would allow me to better the lives of so many other people. So I adopted that as my passion.

That was a complete lie (Lie No.1).

My reasoning made sense to me and the other people with whom I shared that propaganda. The things I really wanted to do, such as uncovering the beauty in people and helping them live their absolute best life, seemed so shallow by comparison—a "nice-to-have," at best. I questioned whether anyone really needed that particular passion (Lie No. 2).

Moreover, I felt as if I couldn't be wildly successful in my passion. I thought I had to be successful in some other field, and doing so would then afford me the freedom to live out my true passion (Lie No. 3). The real estate and other ventures, while total blessings in many respects, were all areas I felt somewhat comfortable. Other people seemed impressed by my achievement. The pursuits felt conventional.

But they never felt *right*.

There are some people who simply have a passion for making money, starting and selling businesses, or the art of the deal, and they are completely unattached to their occupational vehicle. It doesn't matter if they're making money developing real estate, trading stocks or selling cat toilets on the Internet; those pursuits are equally satisfying if the money is right. I tried to adopt that mindset because I thought it was the path of least resistance. In actuality, it turned out to be the path of most resistance for me.

The one thing I can promise about passion, destiny, purpose and all its synonyms is that you will know your passion when you land on it. You'll just know. It will feel like the most natural, congruent truth in the world. And the only fear you'll feel is whether or not you'll be able to accomplish it, but you'll know in your gut it's the mountain you were born to climb.

What Are Your Skills and Strengths?

It goes without much conjecture that no matter what you want to accomplish, you need the skill set to be successful. You need to think very strategically about your current skills and any gap. If you're considering anything entrepreneurial, you not only need the skill for the product or service you want to provide, but also the skill for *building a business* with that product or service. Those are two distinctly different skill sets.

A former client was in law school and interning at a small law firm. One day, she was fuming at her assigned attorney. She declared she would never work for anyone else, and as soon as she passed the bar exam, she was opening her own immigration practice. She was dead serious, too.

I calmly demonstrated the skill gap between where she was and where she needed to be before hanging up her own shingle. There was the process of representing multiple paying clients from start to finish. There was the huge people skill of managing the emotional states of clients who were entrusting her with the immigration status of their loved ones.

There was the skill of balancing her time as an attorney with the responsibilities of being a wife and mother. There was the strategy of marketing and securing clients who not only needed her services but could actually pay for them. That did not include managing the books, billing appropriately or handling collections.

In her own emotional state at that moment, she hadn't fully assessed the skills and strengths required to accomplish her goal, where she was relative to that skills benchmark, or the appropriate timeline and strategy for acquiring those skills. (To be clear, this client is a sharp woman, and she could without question learn all of those necessary skills.)

But to be successful in her passion (and she was totally passionate about this), she had to understand she did not currently possess the experience required to successfully accomplish what she wanted. Once she understood the skills required for all aspects of her goal to open her own practice, then she could determine what investments she should make in training, outsourcing, resources, etc. to close the skills gap.

Most people don't do that kind of self-assessment and end up "winging it," to their detriment.

The passion they are pursuing is not the problem; it's the fact their strategy has not been well-developed in honest evaluation of the gap in their skills and strengths. They have no idea what they are getting themselves into, and they almost always struggle unnecessarily as a result.

What Does the Marketplace Want?

This third element is crucial, and it's where many people fall short. I can't think of anything you could possibly want to do with your life for which there is not a demand somewhere; you simply have to find what and where the demand is.

eBay was built by a man wanting to sell off items around his house. There's a woman on the Internet making six figures selling home-study programs—for quilting. A colleague earns a ton of money teaching people how to become basketball referees. There was even demand for Pee Wee Herman and all his eccentricity. He had his own TV show and movies, for crying out loud! Again, you simply have to find the demand in the marketplace for what you want to do, whether it's entrepreneurial in nature or job-related.

My friend Lauren Solomon is an image consultant based in Los Angeles. The road to

> ### Conversations in the Fast Lane
>
> ✓ Are you truthful about what you really want to do for a living, or do your excuses and doubts snuff out your fire before it ignites?
>
> ✓ Do you believe there is a demand somewhere in the marketplace for what you want to do? How do you know? How can you find out?
>
> ✓ When it comes to your passion, have you ever been a victim of "false positives?" How have they shown up for you?
>
> ✓ What are the most obvious skill gaps you need to fill to pursue your passion? What must you learn or outsource?
>
> ✓ If you're doing work that is "right direction" for you, how easy or difficult has it been to stay authentic to your direction?

her business was a prime example of finding the intersection of your passion and the marketplace. The inspiration to start image consulting came about when she was taking an executive MBA program in the 1990s. She was working for a prominent bank at the time, and the idea came to her as part of a marketing assignment to create her ideal job. When presented with the assignment, she recalls:

> *I DIDN'T KNOW* what it would be, but there had to be something out there. The only thing I loved to do was what I did for my friends when they were getting married—advising them on their hair, styling them, etc. I loved to do something that made people smile. So I went to class and presented image consulting for executives. I asked the question of the class, 'Is this something you might need?' All the hands shot up.

Lauren had to piece her way through, take whatever courses were available and seek the advice of the few who were pioneering the industry. Image consulting was not an established profession at the time.

"I had been practicing what I was learning with my teammates at the bank," she said. "I'd get people to buy me lunch in exchange for a haircut. I would bring in fabrics, eyeglasses, etc. My team was a motley crew within the bank, and some of the team had been passed over for promotions because of the way they looked."

Lauren completely turned around the image, confidence and effectiveness of that team, so much so that she was asked to lead an effort for the entire organization.

"While I was at the bank, I was using my weekends and evenings to do my own thing with the business," she said. "I had incredible productivity levels because I was really excited about what I was doing. I was 35, and I had never experienced that kind of energy."

This was no pipe dream. It was two years of baby steps that took Lauren from "lunch in exchange for a haircut" to the newly created position of vice president of professional image development for the bank she was employed by. Within six years of that first MBA presentation, she left the bank with a full book of clients for her own consultancy. Lauren had found the intersection of her passion and the marketplace.

The battle to stay authentic to your call is a neverending one, as you will learn in subsequent chapters. You will be confronted with the demons of doubt on a regular basis. But when you find that intersection between your passion and the marketplace, those demons don't stand a chance.

Weigh your ego
with your fulfillment
and see which one weighs more.

CHAPTER 19
••••
Uncommon Sacrifices

FAST-LANERS ARE conditioned to always be moving upward and onward. The blessing and curse of finding the joy, fulfillment, peace and exhilaration of "right direction" and the process to get there is contrary to everything we have been programmed to believe as achievers. That programming is laced with so much egocentric nonsense that when we discover the steps we need to take toward greater fulfillment, we realize those steps threaten who we perceive ourselves to be, our identity.

Every fast-laner hits the "what do I do?" crossroad more than once and, in those instances, you must weigh your ego against your fulfillment and see which one weighs more. We introduced a similar concept in chapter 8 and it bears repeating here: When battling ego versus fulfillment, ego usually surfaces as the heavyweight champion, leaving you wondering why, with all your talents, abilities, resources and *(ahem)* good looks, you can't seem to emerge from the mayhem that has become your life.

The issue isn't that you can't emerge. The issue is the price of fulfillment is a pretty hefty one, and the sacrifices required are unlike any you're accustomed to making. If you're really serious about switching to right direction (whatever that is for you), there are three very strategic challenges. If any one of these challenges creates a tightening in your tummy, then I have done my job here.

Challenge No. 1: Be Willing to Take a Step Back to Move Forward

Brenda, a leadership development manager in California, embodied the art of taking a step back in order to move forward, even when she wasn't sure what forward meant.

"When I was in college, I felt that finding the right career path was crucial to me. Everybody has their 'thing,'—things that are most important in their life. For me, I really wanted to find the right career path. I want to do meaningful work that I enjoy and, obviously, pays well. I must feel that I'm using my skills to the utmost, like I am doing the work I was meant to do. That's always been a driving mission for me. I didn't know what that work was when I was in college or through my 20s, and I agonized over it.

"When I hit about 30, I had this epiphany after reading an article written by an alumnus of Georgetown Business School. She had attended a United Nations conference on women in Beijing in 1995, and she wrote an article on her experience. It was like a light bulb came on, and I knew that working to support the advancement of women, ideally globally, was what I really wanted to do. But I didn't know what that looked like. How was I going to use my skills? What do I have to offer? For many years, I went through this intensive self-analysis. How do I manifest my bit on this planet toward the life and success of women?

"When I made the decision to move from fundraising into a leadership development role, I was 39 going on 40 years old. I took the job because I had a lot of volunteer experience in leadership development but no formal experience. I took a job that was knowingly 10 years below my skill set and a huge pay cut just to get the experience. I wasn't even sure that was the area I wanted to be in, so I was in a very exploratory mode.

"I knew going in about the salary cut, but I didn't consider the impact of title changes. I had all these incredible titles previously. I'd always been a director—a senior director, a director of worldwide marketing. I had even been a global director. Now here I am, coming into this job… as assistant director. It had been five years since I'd left the assistant director role, and here I was, going back. That was really brutal and I thought, 'Oh my God, I have to tell the world I'm an assistant director after being senior director?' That was two steps down."

Let's interrupt Brenda's story here. On the surface, her "dilemma" might appear a bit shallow. Tripping over the pay cut we can understand, but the titles? Really? The ego can be *that* shallow. You may not quibble over titles, but how often does ego get in the way of your decisions? How often are you reluctant to ask for help in your marriage, in your spiritual life or with your parenting because you fear what other people will say?

Have you ever been confused about your next step in life, suffering in silence because you don't want other people to know you don't have it all together? When deciding to leave his director of marketing job, my friend Felix recalled, "I didn't want others to perceive I couldn't hack it. And now I don't know who the 'Others' are. I'm not sure if the 'Others' are my friends, my family or that random person on the street. I don't know, but this nebulous 'Others' ruled over me for a very long time."

The "Others" will paralyze you every time. If you are consumed with fear of what other people will think of you, you will fail at Challenge No. 1, a challenge every person must go through in some way to truly get to right direction. You may not have to take a step back in your career or business, but you will have to step back to move forward in some area of your life. I guarantee it. And if you can't get over the "Others," be assured it will take longer than you imagine to get what you truly want.

Fast forward five years later after Brenda's decision to take a lesser job:

> "UNBEKNOWNST TO ME, it set me on the career I was meant to do. I didn't know when I took that job that this is the direction I'd be going five years later. I was in the job, and because it was so below my skill set there were times when I was really bored. There was a voice inside me saying, 'This is not where you're supposed to be. This is not what you're meant to do in this life.' I kept thinking, 'Oh my God! I made the wrong decision. I should have done something else.'
>
> I didn't realize I was actually doing the right work but just at the wrong level. I was incredibly successful at that job, not because I was doing a job that was 10 years below my skills, but because I was naturally good at it. I was naturally good at coaching people. I was naturally good at organizing all kinds of leadership programs. Over time, I realized I was doing what was ultimately my destiny; I just wasn't doing it at the right level."

Brenda is now working for a utilities company doing exactly what she was designed to do and is quite challenged by the work, well-compensated and highly fulfilled. The reason is that she was willing to move in the direction of her goals, even when they weren't quite clear, despite the fact that on the surface some of those steps appeared to be a step backward.

In what areas do you need to take a step back? Jeremy is an investor who had to downgrade his lifestyle to rebuild his finances after a major business setback. Carla had to halt on a business she was building when she realized she had strayed so far from her original vision.

Jessica, a senior sales director for a cosmetics company, chose to sell her house, put all her stuff in storage and move back with her parents when her life spiraled out of control after a bad divorce. She had grown bitter and angry, and was making really bad choices in her life.

"I was so hurt by my ex-husband that I was making really bad choices and thought I needed more accountability in my life," she said. "So, I humbled myself, went to my parents and told them I needed them to be more of a part of my life. I went home for healing; it wasn't for financial reasons. I'm sure a lot of people were like, 'Oh, she has to move back home because her business must be failing.'

"I'm 31 years old and living at home. From the outside looking in, that's super lame. I know that. I'm no fool. But I just have to be confident of who I am and know the reason behind my decision. That's all I really need to know."

Like Jessica, don't let the "Others" keep you from making the crucial decisions that will put you on the path to happiness, healing, joy and true abundance—even if that "Other" is you.

Challenge No. 2: Don't Pooh-Pooh the Small Beginnings

Okay, so the title might be a bit on the juvenile side, but it's no less true. In the fast lane, we tend to want all or nothing—and we want it now. It's not just an issue of the speed with which we want things; it's the warped view that we should go from zero to "freakin' awesome" in anything we attempt to achieve.

I get that many fast-laners have a track record of being at the top of their game: top of the class, captain of the team, leader of the pack, etc., but at some point, we all get to the place where it just doesn't happen as easily or as quickly as we desire. You start taking stock of your life and consider some big change. You consider how long it took to get where you are now and assume this monumental new shift is going to take equally as long. In those moments, one of three scenarios occur:

1.) You work like mad to accelerate your success by setting these aggressive and artificial milestones. You put undue pressure on yourself that creates stress, damages your health, ruins your relationships and makes you an all-around miserable person in the process. You might actually hit your goal, but it's at a tremendous personal cost;

2.) You may end up like most who don't really achieve the success they're capable of because they're inconsistent with the small beginnings. You do some work, look for the big windfall, and when you don't see it (because you may not in the beginning), you move to the next vehicle to accomplish your goal. You show contempt for the small wins—the sprouts of accomplishment in the new business, the gig you conducted for free or the opportunity to volunteer in your desired field—because volunteering doesn't have all the pizzazz you're accustomed. As a result, you don't stick with the journey long enough to arrive at your right direction;

3.) You don't attempt to make the shift at all. Your ego can't handle starting from scratch.

You may disagree with scenarios 2 and 3 because evidence in your life may indicate the contrary: you'll work the long hours, sacrifice your playtime and do whatever it takes. You're no quitter. But consider this: your past accomplishments happened because you had a reasonable sense that your efforts would pay off and that gave you enough confidence to go for the goal.

It's *reasonable* that you can pass the bar exam; countless people have done it before you by doing some common, proven steps. It's *reasonable* that you can get promoted if you nail this next project; you have some level of certainty about that.

But when it comes to finding your "right direction," whether it's a professional direction or a personal/lifestyle shift, the monkey wrench is you rarely have complete certainty that what you're pursuing is actually the right direction. That's what makes right direction so hard to follow. Plus, there are often relatively few examples of people who've actually accomplished *your* right direction. There are few examples of people who want to express their lives in the same way you do. There are few examples of people who have made exactly the same leap you want to make with your exact circumstances.

Although many of your past accomplishments are applause-worthy, the conditions aren't the same as when you are going after your right direction. When you're following *that* right direction, you will consistently question whether you're making the right choices, whether you should turn back and whether it's worth all this dramatic change. That lack of certainty is precisely why scenarios 1, 2 and 3 occur.

The way to avoid these scenarios is to embrace the small beginnings. I once heard Peak Performance coach Tony Robbins say, "People overestimate what they can accomplish in a year and underestimate what they can accomplish in a decade." That's so true. I had the nerve to think I could complete this entire book (yeah, *this one*) in 14 days! 18 months later, I wondered what kind of fast lane crack was I smoking?

Whatever you're trying to accomplish in life, be comfortable with the small beginnings you achieve through consistent action—that's the only thing that is sustainable.

If you recall Lauren Solomon's story in chapter 18, her road to success was about small beginnings. Remember, it was two years of baby steps that took Lauren from "lunch in exchange for a haircut" to vice president of professional image development for her company. Within six years of that first MBA presentation, she left the bank with a full book of clients in her own consultancy. That's the power of small beginnings done consistently.

On the other hand, a more common occurrence came from a coaching client who was a budding real estate investor. In a particular week, she made 30 offers on properties, a volume she had never ever achieved before. My client was disappointed because none of the offers materialized into a contract. She missed the fact that she had placed offers on *30 properties,* a huge accomplishment for any new investor. But she also missed the fact you cannot get to a closed deal without having developed the system of bidding on loads of properties; one precedes the other. She needed to be coached on the value of the small beginnings.

Part of the reason for her dismay was she had been a multiple six-figure earner in her previous career, so that was her benchmark for success. It was initially very difficult for her to embrace the small beginnings of placing offers with no closed deals, so she often struggled with fits and starts in her business. She was a classic case of Scenario No. 2.

You certainly don't have to be a high-income earner to fall into one of these scenario traps, but, ironically, people who are less achieving (by societal standards) fall into these traps far less often. The reason is that people who have less means financially, educationally and otherwise, tend to be overjoyed by their small beginnings. As a result, their gratitude and momentum breeds success more quickly because their actions are *consistent*. Fast-laners, on the other hand, tend to view their small beginnings with more contempt. They want to hurry up and get to the good stuff and, as a result, end up being fast lane, wrong direction far longer than necessary.

This mindset is not relegated to our professional pursuits, either. We do the same thing when it comes to losing weight, fixing a broken relationship or eating healthier. We don't appreciate the small victories, nor do we understand the deeper benefit the small beginnings provide for our personal growth. The great irony is if you can't find joy, peace and fulfillment in the small beginnings of your goal, you won't experience joy, peace or fulfillment even after you've accomplished the goal. Then you'll really be pissed.

Challenge No. 3: Become Obligated to Your Own Happiness
Money is the biggest excuse people use for why they can't live a life of purpose. The close runner-up is not having time. Of course, time presents a problem for many of us because we have real priorities to juggle such as work, family, etc., but an even bigger reason is we obligate ourselves to things we have no business doing. Edward shared his take on obligations:

"I think people-pleasing drives actions that aren't necessarily congruent with your purpose," he said. "You're doing it because you want to be nice. Somebody asked me to sit on a board. I did it because I wanted to be nice, because I didn't want to say no. But I didn't have the passion. I really didn't want to do it.

"All that being nice does is cloud your own priority system because you find yourself trapped, trying to tackle obligations that really are not congruent with the person you are trying to be. In the end, it drives you in one of two ways: either you no longer have the capacity to achieve some of the things you desire to achieve because now you've utilized your energy elsewhere, or it eventually drives you to not being so nice.

"For example, I could be dating a woman because she's a nice person and I want to be a nice guy. Our relationship should really be over, but I don't want to break up with her because I'm being nice. In the end, either it's going to prevent me from finding the woman that I want to be with or it drives me to lead her on. So in the end, I really end up not being 'nice.'"

How many times do you find yourself caught in obligations that just plain suck? You know you're the wrong person to be doing a project and you know you have little interest in the work. But you do it anyhow because you think you should, others expect it of you, or you expect it will satisfy some egotistical need you have for the limelight.

Get over yourself!

Time is a precious commodity and you must guard it with fervor, using your time pri-

> ## Conversations in the Fast Lane
>
> ✓ Judging by your actions, if you were to weigh your ego with your fulfillment, which one would weigh more?
>
> ✓ Is there any area of your life where you feel you need to step back to move forward personally or professionally?
>
> ✓ When considering a major shift in your life, have you ever fallen victim to one of the three scenarios discussed in this chapter?
>
> ✓ How have you responded to your personal or professional small beginnings in the past? Does your perspective need to change in any way moving forward?
>
> ✓ Are you obligating your time to activities that don't fulfill? Is there something you need to cut out?

marily for the activities that coincide with your life's most important values. That doesn't mean you revert to the extreme of selfishness, but it does mean you focus on the activities that grant you the greatest return on fulfillment.

The same goes for your kids. Do you really need to enroll little Susie in seven different weekly activities, especially if she isn't overjoyed about any of them? As a hurry-up society with too many options, we have got to wake up and evaluate how we're spending our time.

I used to serve the American Cancer Society, driving cancer patients to and from their radiation and chemotherapy appointments. I started doing this after my mother was diagnosed with breast cancer, and it was an effective way to give back to something for which I was personally affected. This effort was great for a while until I realized I really didn't enjoy it, even though the cause was noble.

I didn't hate it because I met some fascinating people, and for a couple of hours I was able to grace another person's life. But there were other service opportunities that gave me greater fulfillment, and transporting patients could take two or more hours out of my day. Just because I had the time didn't mean volunteering is what I should be doing with that time.

I challenge you to do an audit of how you are committing your time, whether it's extracurricular activities on the job, in a place of worship, at your child's school, in your recreation or social calendars. Ask yourself why you're doing what you're doing and what's the real return on fulfillment. If something doesn't grade high on the bar of what you value, get rid of that activity. It's time to make your sacrifices meaningful.

When you don't know
where you are going or how to get there,
that's not the time to act "educated."
That is the time to get stupid.
Real stupid.

CHAPTER 20
····
Uhh… You Need Help

SOMEWHERE ALONG THE road to success, many of us picked up the notion we are supposed to navigate life on our own. We're supposed to come up with all the good ideas, make all the right connections, have the perfect marriage, craft the perfect body, raise perfect kids and, all the while, remain in our right minds.

All. By. Ourselves.

We've been deceived big time, and many are suffering unnecessarily in our businesses, careers and home life—on an island all by ourselves—watching our money, time, joy and sense of self-worth wash away with the tide. We see biographies of the "self-made millionaire," not realizing there is no such thing. Many notable people we praise as independent are some of the most dependent people in the world, though it might devalue their stock in the market of public opinion to admit so.

"One of the biggest challenges is people will make all types of mistakes at work," said Tim, who used to be a senior consultant for a major consulting firm. "They wait until the last minute to ask for help because they are afraid of looking dumb. When it's all said and done, they get managed out, and the primary reason they get managed out is because they could have asked for help, but they didn't feel comfortable doing so. I wish I could say the number of times I saw that scenario unfold. For me, that is the No. 1 challenge I see for people—they need to know that it doesn't make you weak to need help."

Tim's right, and here's the kicker: most people actually *like* to help you. People don't like to be used. People don't like to be manipulated. People don't like to be snowballed, but they *do* like to help. People will get you where you want to go faster than you could by yourself, and when you're trying to find right direction in your life, you need more help than you realize.

You need clarity. You need strategies. You need options. You need connections. You need support. You need cheerleaders. You need people to reinforce that you're not crazy. You need people to bear with you when you *are* crazy. You need people to validate your thought process. You need people to challenge your thought process. You need people to open doors. You need people to help you "pick up your face" when doors close. You definitely need people to serve as inspiration during the dark times and, like it or not, you will have lots of dark times on the "right direction" journey.

Get Stupid

I'm a strong believer we can have almost anything we want—as long we're clear about the definition of that "anything" and we are willing to do what it takes to get it. That includes asking for and receiving help. Asking and receiving require a level of humility most people are unwilling to muster because they fear others may think less of them.

Let's be honest: How you perceive me at times is more important than who I really am. If I take the risk to be open, real and vulnerable, your perception of me could change—and not for the better. But vulnerability is essential to finding the right direction for your life. In reality, vulnerability is hard work. But it also takes a lot of emotional and physical energy to fake it, and the energy you're wasting to fake it could be used to actually get what you want.

When talking about achieving what you want out of life, my colleague Evelyn says:

> "IT'S THE POWER of networks and relationships with people, and I also think it is a degree of comfort in not feeling like you have to have all the answers or that you have to shine all the time. It's having a degree of confidence and self-worth even when you're not the smartest person in the room. Even when you're confused, you don't have to feel the pressure to be disingenuous.
>
> When I was transitioning into the education space, I had never been a teacher. I didn't really know anybody in this space, so I had endless conversations with people that I knew well and some that I was meeting for the first time. I would say, 'This is something I think I'm interested in, that I know I believe in. I don't know how to get involved. I don't know how to have impact. What should I do? What books should I read? What classes should I go to? Who else should I talk to?'
>
> It was certainly a pursuit of information," she continued, "but to a degree, it was being aware of my own ignorance and not being afraid to articulate to someone else that I don't know what I'm doing, and I don't know what I'm talking about. But I have a lot of heart, a lot of passion and I think I'm pretty smart. So if you give me some information and point me in the right direction, I think I can probably do some good here."

Evelyn demonstrates what it means to "get stupid," to be a learner, no matter how many degrees or how much experience you may have amassed. If you're not comfortable getting stupid in the areas of your life you need to change, rest assured you will not change.

It's important to make a key distinction from Evelyn's comments. I'm not talking about going on a fact-finding mission and doing some "informational interviews." Most of us have been taught to do that in Guidance Counseling 101. I'm talking about asking for *h… he… help*—with your career, your business, your marriage, your weight, with anything.

Help.

Benjamin recounts his childhood lesson on asking for help:

> **"MY DAD TAUGHT** taught all us kids that the most powerful way to get people to do what we want them to do is to say, 'I was really hoping I could get your help with this.' It's asking for help instead of asking people to do something for you. Showing up and being open and honest is often the ultimate call for help. It's putting you out there saying, 'Here is what I'm struggling with.' The natural response from people will be to introduce you to someone or give you some advice. **"**

Again, people like to help. They like to share what they know, feel a part of someone else's growth. When is the last time you asked for help? The I-don't-have-a-clue-what-I'm-doing kind of help or the I-think-I-know-what-I'm-doing-but-I-could-be-wrong conversations. Truth is, if you've found yourself in the fast lane going in the wrong direction for a while now and you don't have a clue what you're doing, it's probably time to call in the cavalry.

George recalls leaving his job after 21 years to pursue bigger dreams:

"When you're making really good money, have a high level of security and are about to disturb that, there is a tremendous amount of fear within you. I hired a coach for a whole year to help me through that process. And even so, when I wrote the letter giving them notice, I was still terrified."

George may have been terrified when he wrote the letter, but he wrote it, and now he is a successful radio host and relationship coach in New York. As George illustrates, sometimes you have to pay for the help you need; it won't always come from friends, family or mentors.

I highly advocate paying for help because you are essentially paying for speed—whether it's speed to drop the weight, get your business up and running or repair your marriage. Investing in speed is a principle that has catapulted my life in every way imaginable.

> ## Conversations in the Fast Lane
>
> ✓ Do you believe that, at their core, most people like to help?
>
> ✓ When you ask for help, do you typically come from a place of vulnerability or do you project having it all together?
>
> ✓ How do you feel knowing that some people will and some people will not want to help you? Judging by your actions, how much do you care?
>
> ✓ When it comes to lending assistance, do you treat others as you would want to be treated?
>
> ✓ Is there anything in your "spirit of generosity" to others that needs to change?

Some Will, Some Won't

I once heard a speaker say, "Some will. Some won't. So what? Who cares?" That statement changed how I view a lot of things, especially asking for help.

There are three obstacles that keep you from asking for help. The first is you. The second is, well… you. The third is the fear people won't be willing to help you, that you'll be viewed as a nuisance or an intrusion on their time. If you think about it, that fear goes back to you, too. So all three obstacles essentially come down to *you*.

Like it or not, when you reach out for help, you'll find that some people will love you and what you stand for; some will totally dismiss you. Some people will bend over backwards to support and assist you; some will go out of their way to hinder you. Some people will provide constructive feedback to better you; some will mercilessly criticize.

Some people will. Some people won't. That's a reality.

Yes, it will hurt. Choose to get over it. This is one of those rules of life that you simply must accept. What's really cool about accepting this rule is that once you do, you tend to attract more of the people who love you, love your dream, provide constructive feedback for your betterment, cheer on your success and pick you up from your little failures.

Do Unto Others

The biggest question you must ask yourself as you grapple with asking for help is: How willing are you to help others?

Many people find themselves on the fast lane going in the wrong direction because they are takers. They ask-ask-ask, take-take-take, but if someone asks of them, they're unwilling to share their knowledge. Sooner or later (and sometimes never), we come to realize we live in a world of abundance.

My success is not at your expense. If you have more happiness in your marriage, it doesn't mean there's less left for me to enjoy. If you lose 25 pounds, it doesn't mean I'm stuck being 25 pounds heavier. But many of us view life from the lens of scarcity and, as a result, we are unwilling to help those around us.

I'm not saying you take on every person who asks to be mentored. Nor should you say "yes" to every request or give away your talent and money indiscriminately. Instead, consider how you can support, elevate and promote the people around you, whether that's providing a connection or giving advice over the phone. Essentially, do unto others as you would have them do unto you. You know, "The Golden Rule." If you want to get super philosophical, I can insert "what goes around comes around," reaping and sowing, karma kick, but I trust you get the message.

The truth about doing everything yourself is you can't do it yourself. Doing it yourself doesn't work for the long haul—not in business, the workplace, your marriage or with your kids. When you pretend you can do it all, other people will eventually believe you can; it will not occur to those able and willing to assist you in reaching your goals to consider offering help.

Your unwillingness to ask for help will train people that you don't need help, and when you need help most, you will perceive that people don't want to help. That is because they assume you don't need assistance, making this a self-defeating cycle.

It's no accident that you go through
some dark places on the way to your goal.
It's those dark places that transform you into the
person you need to be to get what you want.
Don't hate on the dark place.

CHAPTER 21
••••
Dark Places

FINDING RIGHT DIRECTION in your life is about more than taking a leap of faith. You've got to be strategic about this journey and know what to expect so you don't get caught off-guard.

I occasionally share with people my fear of flying. I've been flying since I was 4 years old, and up until my early 30s, I flew without fear. Then, I developed this unexplainable fear of flying. Turbulence terrified me, and any little ripple of the wings would have me praying for calm winds. What I found interesting is I was fine if the pilot came on the intercom and said, "We're expecting some choppy air ahead, so I'm turning the 'fasten your seatbelt' sign on for the next 20 minutes."

But I got all sorts of freaked out if the plane dipped without warning, and the seatbelt sign popped on suddenly. The difference is I knew what to expect in the first scenario, and regardless of the circumstance, I felt as if the pilot had everything under control.

That's why I wrote this chapter, so you would know what to expect as you make your transition to right direction. There will be some dark places in your journey. If you don't know what to expect, you could get so discouraged by the discomfort of those places that you chuck it all and head back to your safe zone, whether that safe zone is being mired in work, staying single and uncommitted, or remaining undesirably overweight.

You would be safe, but you would be miserable.

You see, the dark places are about the refinement of your dreams and the refinement of the dreamer. It's in the dark places that you actually learn how to switch lanes. In the dark places you're often not sure of what you want or where you're going, even though you may have felt certain just a little while before. You're in that place where you lack focus and clarity.

In the dark places, you'll have tough conversations with people you love who won't necessarily understand why you are making the decisions you're making, whether it's to be the stay-at-home parent or forgoing that graduate degree. You'll feel alone and foolish at times. You'll wonder why you didn't turn back long ago.

You will be deeply challenged in the dark places. Your identity will be tried, and you will have to honestly answer the question of who you are without your most prized possession—your ego. The challenge could be as simple as not knowing what to say after being laid off or the feeling of failure for your business taking so long to get going or being confused about the direction of your personal life. The challenges will be very real.

I don't know the specifics of the dark places for you (and no, not everybody loses all their money as I did), but the dark place is coming and it will often arrive than once. The gift of the dark place is that it squeezes out the very qualities in you that keep you from experiencing immense joy, vitality, love and freedom in your life. Whatever needs to get refined will be refined in the dark places, but only if you have the courage to embrace the process. The problem is, when people encounter their dark places, they assume it means they have messed up. That couldn't be further from the truth; they're actually right on path.

Whenever you make a shift, whether it is a complete U-turn in your life or merely changing lanes, you have to step through that proverbial "wall of fear." Everyone does.

Making that step is a major breakthrough and there's great relief as you recognize the fear of the other side is far worse than the actuality of the other side. When you're stepping through the wall to your right direction, there's usually some immediate reward, like a confirmation that you're on the right path. It feels like a form of "beginner's luck," such as securing your first business deal or hitting a bull's eye your first go-around at the shooting range.

When I started life coaching, I launched the business by hosting my own half-day seminar. There were naysayers who discouraged me from doing it that way, insisting I start small and build up. But I went ahead nonetheless, and it was a fantastic event. Soon after, I started securing TV appearances and thought, "Whoo-hoo! Why didn't I step up sooner? This is great!"

Little did I know the challenges that lay ahead and, honestly, had I known what I was getting into, I might have withdrawn my application from the "Life to the Full Club!" What enabled me to persist, however, was I prayed—a lot. I stayed glued to coaches and mentors. I fueled on books and audios that warned me to expect challenges, to understand their purpose and to reframe them.

However, no book revealed that as an achiever, my drive, ego and identity—not my challenges—were the biggest obstacles to my happiness. Those realizations didn't come when I first left my day job and pursued my "dreams." Those realizations came in the dark places. No matter how hard I worked, how much I invested or how carefully I strategized, until I was refined on the inside, I could not experience true success and happiness. That's why *Fast Lane, Wrong Direction* is focused so much on *you* looking at *you*.

So what should you do after stepping through the wall of fear into your right direction and you recognize things are beginning to turn dark? Things aren't going according to plan after an initial buzz. In these moments, you must learn to manage the confusion, or you will turn tail and run back to whatever safe circumstance you came from. You cannot listen to the "noise in your head."

> "It's very easy to self-destroy everything
> you created when you are in that moment of fear.
> It's easy to turn around and give up, but you have to stay the course."
> —Nathan, founder, www.SoulNeeds.com

> "I believe you cannot be in a successful, growing business
> without having the thought of, 'OMG—what if it falls apart next week?'"
> —Gary, business owner

In the dark places, you will second-guess your direction incessantly, like a million times a week. It may feel as if you're hearing five different voices in your mind at the same time. That's because you are. There's your momma telling you to be safe, your best friend wondering if you're making the right choice, and don't forget the three split personalities in your head, each with an opinion of their own!

Image consultant Lauren Solomon shared one of her dark place experiences when her business collapsed as a result of the 9/11 terrorist attack on the World Trade Center:

"I left the bank to do my business full time in 1999. In January 2000, I outlined my book with my girlfriends. I started to write the book, then was offered an exclusive contract with another big bank. I put the book on the shelf and was inside of the corporate environment again and felt the energy of the corporate space.

"Then September 11th happened, and my business was in the World Trade Center. All my clients survived, but my business was gone. I was the president of the Association of Image Consultants at the time. I was thinking to myself, 'Image consulting is so superficial.' I had 800 associate members in 30 companies and I was sitting right in the middle of the storm.

"So in six weeks, I went back and wrote that book. In six months, I had it published. The title was *Image Matters*. Image matters in a crisis and when things go wrong. That experience changed my direction, even though I was in the right direction. It brought a different level of humanity to my book.

"I also learned we've got to be real every step of the way because every single person who has been successful has likely been at the bottom. And they've been there more than once. They have to be willing to tell you about it. Otherwise, this life could just be a constant run toward suicide if you don't understand this is how success usually works."

Like Lauren, I went through a pretty dark place after one of my businesses failed, and for a couple of years, I was barely getting by. In my mind, my big break was always "just around the corner," so it took a while for me to realize just how broke I had become and *how long* I'd been that way.

Maybe the reason for my denial is during that dark season, money would come just in the nick of time to pay my bills; a deal would close or an opportunity would open up. It was not until I decided to short sale my house and subsequently qualified for my county's moderate income housing program (because my income the previous year had been so low) that it clicked, "Uhh...chick, you're pretty broke."

Unless you've had a dream or goal you were committed to against all rationale, you might not relate to what I'm sharing. I mean, how do you *not* realize you're broke? In retrospect, I think I realized it; I just didn't accept it. Something inside kept saying I was going in the right direction, even though I wasn't bearing the financial fruit from my efforts.

I had blown through my savings, blown through my retirement and incurred a fair amount of debt from the businesses. My right direction at that point seemed utterly wrong. The rational, responsible woman I was reputed to be on the outside felt like a complete failure and a total idiot on the inside. But as scared and uncomfortable as I was in that dark place, I couldn't bring myself to turn back.

I later learned there was a reason....

The irony of the dark place is that it is less about the achievement of your goal as it is about who you get to become in the pursuit of that goal. There are plenty of people who have what you think you want—the marriage, money, prominence, kids, travel—and are still unhappy, so there must be more to happiness than the achievement of the "thing." And that's where the dark place comes in. For Lauren Solomon, the dark place changed how she viewed her work and the value she added to her clients.

For me, it was something different. There were times during my journey when I had $200,000 in the bank, and there were times when I had $1.97. I was broke at $1.97, but I was *broken* at $200,000. Being broken had nothing to do with money or greed. Being broken had to do with all the fast lane, wrong direction stuff we have discussed throughout this book; I was broken on the inside. At $1.97, I was in a pretty dark place financially, but there was a gift in that place I never expected.

At $1.97, I developed faith to stay in my right direction despite circumstances that suggested otherwise. At $1.97, I developed the courage to see my value and worth independent of my trophies. At $1.97, I learned to actually enjoy life, something I never truly did when I was "successful." It was a long, dry, barren season, but eventually the tide shifted, and the reward for making it through was better than I ever could have imagined. Unbeknownst to me, the gifts awaiting me in the dark places were the very reasons why I could never turn back.

Regardless of their pedigree, every one of my clients goes through a dark place where they question their direction and whether or not they have what it takes to get through to the other side. Had I not gone through my dark places, I wouldn't be able to witness the warning signs or provide perspective to my clients in the way that I do. I grasp my clients' fears and the glitches in the matrix of their thinking. Because of that, they invest in me to help them speed through and bypass the unnecessary pain and delay they would otherwise experience.

I will go through some dark places again. They will be different circumstances, different players and different lessons. It may be personal instead of professional, a health challenge instead of a financial one, but it will come again. Because I realize the dark places are "par for the course," and that the "course" is bigger than me and my personal happiness, I will be able to have a productive perspective as I go through them.

Whatever the right direction is for you and regardless of the goal, those root issues we covered—identity theft, the fraud syndrome, need for speed, etc.—will get handled in the dark places. The dark places will ensure you don't do all the hard work to drop 50 pounds only to later ask, "Is this all there is?"

The dark place is your gift. It doesn't feel like it, but it is, and if you allow the dark places to do their work, you will emerge with an increased freedom, vitality, peace and zest for life like you've never known. Over time, however, you will learn to better navigate the dark places, learn your lessons more quickly and reduce the time of your growth spurt.

Here are a few suggestions when you find yourself in a dark place:

1.) Find Your Faith

I do not aim to tell you what to believe spiritually; each man must walk that journey for himself. I can only share what has worked for me, and an integral part of my success has come by faith.

There is absolutely no way I would have triumphed over my dark places without a real, genuine, trusting faith—faith there was a purpose for my life, a purpose to my challenges and a future outcome that was better than my current circumstances. I thought I had faith when I started my right direction journey, but I soon came to realize it was "intellectual faith," not a tried-and-true, refined-by-fire kind of faith.

There were so many times I wanted to turn back. There were so many times when my intellect, talents and background weren't enough. There were so many times I felt inadequate and I had to find a confidence that rested in my value before God alone, not the value I perceived when I looked in the mirror. The only thing that kept me from quitting (or having an emotional break) in those seasons was the belief that I was on my God-given purpose, and God's purposes cannot fail.

Personal growth, self-help, positive thinking and peak performance will take you far, but it is faith that will sustain you when all that reaches its limit, and it will. You must find faith for yourself. There's only so much of someone else's you can borrow.

2.) Live Your Mission

Your highest confidence will come from knowing you are living your mission or, at a minimum, following your "passion for now." When you are following that passion for now, it's easier to make sense of the dark place, to recognize its transformative gift, embrace the lessons and speed on through. For Felix, living his mission has made a real difference in his life. He discusses the shift in his confidence level when he left his marketing director role and began pursuing interior design.

> *I WISH I could say I had this 180-degree change, that I'm confident in everything I do, but I struggle with it. What has changed is that I love what I do and I have confidence in what I do. This confidence doesn't come from an external source. It isn't because someone else told me that I was the smartest person in the group or that I had the best 'whatever.' It lies in the fact that I love to cook, I love interior design, I love the event planning aspects of what I do. All that is innate within me. So there is this current center of calmness that I have now.*

As Felix learned, a funny thing happens when you're doing the things you feel called to do and recognize them as your gift: you become more adept at quieting those demons of doubt I mentioned in chapter 18. Your "call" does not have to be CEO of a company; you could simply be leading a Girl Scout troop with your daughter. Whatever it is, all the delays, setbacks, challenges and twists stop being signals of your failure and instead become preparation for your inevitable success. It really does change the game.

3.) Manage the People Who Influence You

In an earlier chapter, we talked about the three types of relationships you want to foster. Relationships are critical when you are in your dark places. When you take your life in a new direction, even if the change seems slight, you will feel very vulnerable. That's totally natural. In that state, surround yourself with people who line up with your way of thinking.

> ## Conversations in the Fast Lane
>
> ✓ When you think about stepping into the "right direction" in some area of your life, how do you react when you consider the dark places you could face?
>
> ✓ Have you gone through dark places in your past and now realize the gift in the challenge?
>
> ✓ What role has faith played in your life to date? What, if anything, needs to change as you look ahead?
>
> ✓ How would living your mission, or your "passion for now," impact your view on the dark places between here and your goal?
>
> ✓ Are there any changes you need to make in your relationships as you consider pursuing your right direction?

They don't have to agree with every choice you make, but they must be people who focus on the possibilities and all the ways you can create the life you want. Avoid those who approach life from a fear-based perspective, especially during your dark seasons. They will suck the life right out of your dream.

4.) Do Steps 1-2-3 Over and Over and Over Again

More likely than not, you have been conditioned for fast lane, wrong direction much of your life, and it's going to require repetition to undo the belief systems and patterns that have you chasing unsatisfying aspirations. You'll get better at making choices that free you, defining an identity unattached to your accomplishments and navigating the dark places. But you must recognize that the temptation for wrong direction never truly goes away.

Wrong direction loses its pull over time, but it will always feel like your safest option, and that's why it is so dangerous. Pride is always safer than humility. Pretending you have it all together is always safer than admitting you don't. Conducting work you are good at doing and have invested years is easier than learning to do work you love, especially when you're 38 years old with two kids. But should you accept the mission to right direction, there's no end to its rewards.

Remember, it's no accident you go through some dark places on the way to your goal. It's those dark places that transform you into the person you need to be for you to actually get what you want… and not screw it up once you have it.

Don't "hate" on the dark place.

"Art is a collaboration between God and the artist,
and the less the artist does, the better."
— Andre Gide

CHAPTER 22
••••
It's Bigger Than You

AT SOME POINT, be it now or later, you'll come to the end of your talent. You'll come to the end of your reason and your connections. Life as you know it won't make sense. You'll come to the end of yourself, and on that precipice you'll start asking the bigger questions about life—those very questions you try to avoid in your busyness but are haunted by in your quiet moments.

Try as you might, you can't escape them.

I've come to the end of myself a few times over the years, and I would wonder, "What the hell is the point and who thought this thing up?" I couldn't understand why it was completely impossible for me to be satisfied with my salary. I couldn't understand why I felt so discontent even though I had more than enough to be comfortable. I had good moments and fun times and cool experiences, but I couldn't shake the fact that my spirit just didn't feel *satisfied*. I felt like the most ungrateful person walking.

And then there was God.

You may have some resistance to the "G" word, and that's okay. Just stick with me. From the moment I started writing, I wondered how to incorporate God into a success book, yet I knew without a doubt I couldn't write the book without doing so. I imagine you've figured out by now that I'm a very flawed person with loads of shortcomings, so I'm in no position to dictate what you should believe in your own spirituality.

I do, however, believe that our view of God—whatever that is—profoundly affects our perspective on our fast lane experiences, so avoiding the God topic in an effort to be politically correct, in my opinion, leaves a sizable missing piece in the "right direction" puzzle.

Most advisors to this project suggested I not touch this topic with a 10-foot pole, but if you've learned anything about me to this point, you know I'm so gonna "go there!"

I openly share that my faith in God is the "secret sauce" in my recipe of success and fulfillment in the fast lane, but that does not have to be the case for you to benefit from all we discussed in the previous chapters. In the next few pages, I will share spiritual principles and perspectives that have transformed my fast lane pursuit, and you are free to determine whether or not those principles will become essential ingredients in your own right direction recipe.

In the United States, there is a neverending effort to separate church and state, or in the broader context, religion and government. While that makes sense to protect the civil liberties of a nation comprised of differing belief systems, I assert that you cannot separate your personal faith (in whatever you believe) from your talent, dreams, goals or any other aspect of your "fast lane, right direction" pursuit. They are inextricably linked. If you believe this or that about God, it affects how you pursue right direction. If you profess to have no belief in God at all—that, too, affects how you pursue right direction. Contrary to what most of us assume, this is one area we cannot compartmentalize.

As was the intent with the preceding chapters, I hope this chapter challenges you. Specifically, I hope it encourages you to explore your position on your own faith and evaluate how that position serves you—positively, negatively or in between—as you navigate your fast-lane journey.

Wherever you land on the intersection between God, fast lane, wrong or right direction is your personal business. There are few easy questions in this regard, and the answers are often hard to swallow. I simply encourage you to be brave enough to explore the connection.

It's Bigger Than You

I like to think of myself as a fairly smart cookie, but smart as I was, for a whole decade I couldn't rationalize my way into loving my work. For over a decade, no amount of praying, reading the Bible and going to church could bring me out of the ever-subtle funk I felt about the direction my life was headed. I was missing something pretty fundamental; I just didn't know what it was. I tried and tried and tried, with all objective logic and spiritual platitudes, to be satisfied with the life I had, yet it felt as if the decisions I was making were in complete opposition to the very core of my being.

I was grateful, but I honestly wasn't happy. I wanted to be content, and if I could have clicked my heels and made it so with the life I had, I would have—gladly. But there was this involuntary disturbance, as if forces were working against me, even in the "good" times. Turns out, there was a force at work all those years, yet it wasn't working against me; it was working *for* me.

Remember our friend Jacob, the one who jumped out of the moving taxi from chapter 1? He shared his perspective on God at what proved to be one of his darkest times:

"I did not believe in God because… how the hell could this happen to me if there was a God? I was a victim through and through."

Jacob went on to accomplish some fairly extraordinary feats, and his perspective on God took a complete "180" turn in subsequent years. His perspective changed so much that he later conceded, "If you try to do this leap of faith to success without God, you're going to find yourself messed up." I agree with Jacob.

Without a realization that there is something bigger than you and your limitations, it's difficult to break free of the fast lane trappings. The incessant need for speed, the fears of failure and the inability to stand up for your life are driven by an unconscious belief that you are somehow on your own, that you're controlling the show, and as the old adage goes, "if it is to be, it is up to me."

To relinquish the death grip you have on your life and begin to enjoy the freedoms of your authentic "right direction" in life, love, career and everything else, you must come to the realization that your life, success and even your happiness is bigger than you.

Yes, it's bigger than you.

The fact you may be in the fast lane going in the wrong direction right now is bigger than you. The challenges you face are bigger than you. Your life purpose is bigger than you, as is your "passion for now." The pain and frustration you feel is—you guessed it—bigger than you. And until you grasp that it's bigger than you, it will always be *about* you, and you'll never quite find right direction.

In fact, relatively few people do.

Finding right direction is hinged on understanding that you have been uniquely designed to make a positive difference in the lives of people around you. Your sphere of influence may be 10, 10,000 or 10 million. When you finally understand that everything from your painful childhood to your recent divorce to failing the bar exam three times before finally passing all contribute to your ability to live out your God-given purpose. You will be able to impact people in ways you never conceived. Then you will be ready for rock star-level fulfillment.

You recognize that you, with all your quirks, preferences, bents and leanings, are an ingenious creation after all (otherwise known as "pretty hot stuff!"). Suddenly, pursuing your authentic success takes on a new meaning as you realize there are people you've never met who are waiting… for your book to be released, for your product to launch, for your blog to post, for you to lose weight, for you to find balance, for you to repair your marriage, for you to take the helm of that new department and steer it in a more altruistic direction.

They need your story of triumph because your story of triumph will inspire theirs.

You will begin to take notice of your cheerleaders, whether they are your kids or your entire community, and you'll notice there are cheerleaders all around you. Their need for you becomes proof that whatever "it" is, it's bigger than you. When you allow your life to be bigger than you, God steps in. When God steps in, He starts to reveal how all the "forces" in your life are working *for* you, not against you, as they have been all along.

And that's when magic happens.

The magic I'm talking about isn't some mythical force that controls your destiny, requiring no work or input on your part. If that were the case, you could skip all the preceding chapters and merely let "God's plan" take over!

No, the magic happens when you become skilled at processing what shows up in your life, what appears good, what appears bad and what appears ugly. The bad is often good in disguise. The good is usually even better than you believe. And the ugly… well, that's the stuff dreams are made of down the road. You just can't see it at the time.

Lucky Enough to Lose

We rarely view it this way, but most of us get lucky enough to lose a lot in our lives. We lose the love we thought was "The One," only to rebound years later with the man or woman we couldn't imagine living without. We get punched in the gut, metaphorically, our dreams get shattered and our progress feels stalled. It sucks. It really, really *sucks*. The million-dollar question is whether it sucks because we lost what we wanted or because we didn't realize we were lucky enough to lose it.

I was "lucky enough to lose" all those years I was miserable with my work. I didn't see it at the time, obviously, but had I not failed at some of my ventures, I would still be doing work I hate. I had such a warped criteria for success, and I had no qualms with killing my spirit to attain that success. I was lucky enough to lose, but it was more than that.

The misery I experienced chasing the proverbial carrot on a stick has shaped my entire coaching and motivational speaking platform. I wouldn't be writing this book were it not for those experiences, and I would not be able to navigate my coaching members through the murkiness of strategically designing their own success. Failure ushered me into my destiny and I later realized those losses weren't just about me.

Losing was bigger than me.

For my friend Elenore, getting removed from a very high-profile position held the seeds to an incredible life of balance and fulfillment. Recalling the turn of events from her promotion to her demotion, she shared:

"Because I'm not a risk taker, I allowed the company career path to dictate my life," she said. "I was reporting directly into the CEO, but I had no idea what I was stepping into because I had fallen in love with the image of it all. There's something about me… and it may be my insecurity, but the validation I received when the people I respected and admired the most picked me for that job meant more to me than anything else at that point. Looking back, that wasn't healthy. I should not need my validation from people who, outside of a professional context, had no other import into my life. But the belief they had in me meant everything to me.

"**THE PROBLEM STARTED** started when the boss who hired me for the role left the company," Eleanor continued. "Key staff members quit and everything began to change. In my mind, everything was speeding up and I started questioning whether or not I was capable. Why did I end up in this job? The job was probably legitimately more than I could handle, and as I began questioning my own confidence, things started to go downhill fast. I was not happy nor did I believe I was doing the best job for the business, but I couldn't self-select out because that would be quitting. So I had to keep going.

I truly believe the company did the best thing for the business and the best thing for me by pulling me out of that role. Though I was unceremoniously removed as the head of the department, I am eternally grateful to the company for that moment. That was my moment of clarity. That's when I realized there's a certain professional contract between the company and me, and it's nothing more than that.

When I considered the time I forfeited with my kids and husband, there was a tremendous amount of personal sacrifice that went into keeping up professionally in that role. But when the company needed to make a business decision, it wasn't about personal loyalties, and it shouldn't be. That gave me permission to also manage my relationship with the company as a professional relationship. I chose to work here; I can choose not to. It's nothing more than that.

Deciding to stay at the company after being removed was much harder than running away, and it forced me to look beyond my professional side and plan out my 'life experience,' with the professional being one part of that instead of the whole. I took a different approach to how decisions would be made in my career. I thought about what aspects of my job I really enjoyed and began to craft a new role around that. I found my passion for the company again. I wasn't going to let things be dictated to me, and there was a sense of pride for taking control of my career for the first time.

I landed at the top of the pyramid because I was a slave to what other people thought. That's how I ended up in the wrong lane. It really mattered to me what people thought, and when I was finally willing to let that go, I found my happiness. That was so liberating for me! It became about me taking control over my own happiness and gaining my validation from myself and my family, not from other people."

Elenore was lucky enough to lose. She crafted a new role for herself that has served her well over the years. At the time of our interview, she was telecommuting with the same company, going into the office only one day a week. Her responsibilities dramatically decreased because of the demotion, yet she maintained the same salary with the same title she had at promotion, with far less stress. She has more flexibility than most working women to be present with her family, and family is the most important thing to her.

I hope you recognize that Elenore's experience is about more than how to pick up your face after an embarrassing defeat; this is so much more than a public relations "comeback" story. I believe God handed Elenore an opportunity of a lifetime to live more authentically, a desire she didn't realize she had. She never would have chosen those circumstances, but those are the exact circumstances she needed.

At the time, Elenore could only focus on the "you know what" just hit the fan with her job. But she soon came to realize that for years she was wanting something she didn't really… *want*, and was driving herself mad to get it.

"For me, it was coming to understand who I am and what motivates me instead of living the life I was 'supposed' to lead," Elenore said. "I might not have a second child if it were not for that experience. It allowed me to get back a sense of perspective that was sorely lacking. Then I was able to understand what makes me happy *and* gives me balance. At that moment, it was very much about my kids, and I needed to redefine my professional life so that I was in balance with that. After 19 years, I haven't found an alternative career that would net more in my favor than I have right now."

Interestingly, Elenore is now a go-to person for women, particularly those grappling with how to maintain work/life values. How she makes decisions for herself and for her family, and the level of authenticity with which she makes them, was forever changed by this one experience.

She was lucky enough to lose.

Connecting the Dots

Have you ever taken the time to look back on your life and start connecting the dots? Have you looked beyond what you may perceive to be good or bad right now to piece together the threads: the experiences you had growing up, challenges you overcame, activities that thrilled you and even the ones that bored you to tears?

It's when you start weaving together the tapestry of your past that you truly begin to understand there's really something bigger at play. That realization will give you the courage to step up and take risks you could never imagine with your right direction.

My friend Julie is an incredible person. She went from having a growth disorder in high school where she was so small she had to wear kids' clothes to being a plus-size woman in college. She is an Emmy-nominated TV host for MTV, former Miss Virginia beauty queen, a former senior leadership consultant for the Pentagon and an award-winning speaker. But if you ask Julie what she's all about, she'll simply say, "I help kids."

Julie knows a few things about connecting the dots.

"WHEN I WAS in high school, I had a growth disorder," she said. "Even though I was a sophomore, I was so short and so small I looked like I was in the fifth grade. To top that off, I had a really high, squeaky voice. Whenever I talked, people would snicker, so needless to say, high school was not much fun for me.

We all have those moments we would call turning points, and my turning point was a school assembly. I remember going down to the assembly with a really negative attitude. I think someone had called me a nerd in the hallway, and I was feeling pretty bad. When the door opened for the assembly, in walked this 6-foot-3 African-American man. He was bald and wearing this beautiful tuxedo. It just caught my attention. It wasn't so much what he was wearing; it was the way he was carrying himself and the energy he was radiating as he walked across the gym floor.

When he spoke, he said, 'I am wearing my best because you deserve the best. You deserve the best life and you deserve to make the best choices.' What was amazing to me is at that moment I felt like he was talking directly to me. For whatever reason, those words went straight into my soul. I was like, 'You know what? He's right. I deserve to live the best life. It doesn't matter that I come from a family that doesn't have a lot of money. It doesn't matter that kids make fun of me.'

Two things happened that day. One, even though I was 4 feet 7—really small, short and skinny—I walked taller out of that gymnasium. I felt taller. The second thing I remember as I was walking down the hallway is that I thought someday I want to be able to do the same thing for others that person did for me. That's when the seed was planted that I really wanted to work with students. I really wanted to help teens and kids feel good about themselves and understand they have the power to live a great life."

It should come as no surprise that at this stage of her life, Julie didn't have enough "dots" to connect. As genuinely inspired as she was that day, she went on to more conventional academic pursuits, focusing on a pre-veterinary degree at Ohio State. While studying abroad in England, she realized for the first time she wasn't happy on the path she was pursuing. She recalls:

"I was sitting at my desk studying for a huge biology exam, looking at this massive stack of books on human and animal physiology and chemistry thinking, 'Why am I so miserable?' Then it was like the voice of God that said, 'What is a job you love so much that you would do it for free?' I was like, 'Oh my gosh!' It was another a-ha moment. I almost kicked myself!

"I felt so stupid. I couldn't believe it had taken me so long and that I had to go all the way to England to get away from the everyday pressures to realize what the truth was,"

Julie continued. "I loved youth leadership so much that every summer of my college career I lived on credit cards so that I could volunteer at youth leadership conferences. I loved youth leadership so much that I was paying out of my own pocket to have those experiences. If I looked at my electives, they were all leadership-oriented classes that I took on my own just because I loved it. All my volunteer work was youth leadership conferences and camps and things to help girls and kids."

Julie went back to Ohio State after her year abroad, discontinued her pre-vet program and created her own degree program in Leadership Studies. It took her almost six years to graduate, but on that experience she said, "Sometimes it's a winding road to get where you're supposed to be, and as long as you listen to yourself when it's not feeling right and you redirect your path, it ultimately works out for the best."

To fast forward through Julie's story, after graduation she volunteered at a youth leadership conference and met someone who worked for the Pentagon. At that time, a Leadership Studies degree was unusual. Julie ended up being hired to do leadership training and development programs for a division of the Pentagon, at age 23. Yeah, that skinny girl who used to get bullied in school was hired at the headquarters for the U.S. Department of Defense. It was a lot of hard work, and she put in some long hours. Then, not unlike many of us, Julie got sucked into the "fast lane, wrong direction" vortex.

"I got sucked into the Washington D.C., corporate culture where you're making good money and your whole life is work, so I continued at the job much longer than I should have," she said. "I had this 80-hour a week job, and I was exhausted. A heart-to-heart talk with my then-boyfriend helped put things into perspective.

"He said, 'You are killing yourself. You really need to make a choice. Now is the time where you owe it to yourself to get rid of the parts of your life that are not serving you and to move on and live your mission. You lit up when you used to talk about mentoring and being a speaker for kids. You've been saying this for years. Now is the time to do it. If you don't, you're going to lose parts of your life you value most.'

"So I submitted my letter of resignation. I cried because I realized this was the start of what it feels like to have peace. I felt like I was honoring God's plan for my life, and I was freeing up space to focus on taking care of myself and my relationships and building a new career. It was very, very scary, but it was very peaceful and joyful at the same time. I was just sorry I didn't listen to that little voice sooner."

Julie is building an incredible speaking and mentoring business for girls and young women. In addition to the accomplishments mentioned earlier, she recently authored an inspiring book titled *BeYOUtiful*. The accolades can go on forever, but none of that matters because if you ask Julie what she does for a living, she'll tell you, "I help kids."

The pain of the 4-foot-7 teenager with the squeaky voice helps kids. The girl whose life was forever influenced by a confident man in a tuxedo helps kids. The girl who swelled

> ## Conversations in the Fast Lane
>
> ✓ In what ways have you felt that forces were working against you—in love, in life, business or career? Is it possible that God has been working for you? If so, how?
>
> ✓ Do you believe God should play a major, minor or nonexistent role in your life? How does your belief affect your confidence in the direction your life is headed and the ease by which you enjoy the ride?
>
> ✓ When you start connecting the dots in your own life, what does it reveal about your life's purpose or mission?
>
> ✓ How does the view that your life is bigger than you affect your confidence in taking the next steps to live your "right direction?"
>
> ✓ Do you ask God's direction as you make big and small decisions with work, relationships, parenting, etc. Or, do you more often rely on your own ability?

into a plus-size college student a short time later helps kids. The woman that went on to become the Miss Virginia beauty queen… helps kids. She helps kids to believe in themselves as they are, whatever their shape, size or background. She helps them to become leaders of themselves and their communities.

Julie connected the dots.

So What's the Point?

In all my religiosity, I believed God, but I didn't know God. If I really knew God, I would have trusted there was a plan bigger than me that was authentic to my talents, desires, fancies and weird idiosyncrasies, not in opposition to them.

If I really knew God, I could have seen the pain and frustration for the refinement and redirection that it was, instead of fighting to hold my position with people and things I didn't really want anyway. If I really knew God, I could have recognized more immediately how circumstances I perceived to be colossal disappointments held the seeds to some of my greatest blessings. I wasted so much time worried, afraid, anxious and discontent—unnecessarily. Could the same hold true for you?

We cry, complain, curse and shake our fists at the heavens because we don't get what we want, when we want or how we want it. We inflict so much pain on ourselves by clinging uncompromisingly to outcomes we believe *should* happen in our lives, but oftentimes what should happen to us is happening to us; we just don't agree with that fact at the time.

In those moments, we fail to realize how limited our purview on life really is. We think we know what's best for us, but we have no clue what will truly make us happy. The things we think will make us happy leave us feeling flat, and experiences we underestimate on the happiness scale blow us away with joy. Sometimes we are utterly clueless, but God never is.

What I think to be one of the most profound scriptures in the Bible is from Romans 8:28: *"God causes all things to work together for the good of those who love him, who have been called according to his purpose."*

Notice the scripture does not say all things are good, but it does say God causes all things to *work together* for good—our triumphs, our screw-ups, our grief and unexpected detours.

If you take time to connect the dots in your own life, perhaps you can catch glimpses of this principal at work. And if you go so far as to embrace the idea that your life could be bigger than you, that there's a loving God who actually supports your growth and happiness, how much more peace might you enjoy? How much less control would you attempt to exert over everything and everybody (as if that ever worked anyway)? How much more surrender could you have in the everyday circumstances, trusting that when you do your very best, the outcome that is the outcome that should be...it just might take a minute for it all to make sense?

By now you've figured it out fast lane, right direction isn't just about the destination. It's so much more about how you enjoy the ride. And I like to call that realization—a game changer.

I misunderstood my experiences and misread the signs. I didn't recognize that embedded in my DNA is a path of least resistance. Not a path of least hardship, not a path of least tragedy or challenge… a path of least resistance.

CHAPTER 23
••••
You Can Have Much More

I COULD GO on endlessly with testimonials of people who have found right direction in some area of their life by applying one or more of the principles on these pages. This is the conclusion you were waiting for, right? The happily ever after... the fastest way to "done"... the 10 simple steps to your very best life? Jordania, an executive for a research company, sums it up beautifully:

> "I don't think there's anything wrong with a certain contentment or happiness about where you are, without always having to be racing toward something else... taking honest joy in where you are and who you are, the blessings you have and being healthy. I have a good job. I have flexibility. My worst fear is the other shoe is going to fall. This is almost too good! But that's a great place to be."

Jordania's right. That is a great place to be. But getting "there" (and staying there) is your ever-elusive goal. Throughout *Fast Lane, Wrong Direction*, we have covered guiding principles to help you quickly navigate those "wrong direction" periods of your life with the least amount of pain possible. But those principles are not one-time, feel-good motivational moments. To the contrary, the more you condition yourself to live by these simple guidelines, the more powerful the impact these principles will have on your happiness.

We all experience an emotional high at a moment of breakthrough, and I sincerely hope you've had quite a few breakthroughs through the course of our interaction. The mistake is resting on the revelations, making a quick fix or two and thinking that it's smooth sailing thereafter.

Right direction simply doesn't work like that.

Just when you think you've cracked the "right direction" code, something will inevitably happen that challenges your belief in these principles. Why? Because right direction often feels like a test, then another test and another test…and in some ways it actually is. A popular American idiom when expressing gratitude for the service of military personnel is "freedom isn't free." And I imagine you've figured out by now that right direction ain't free either! You've got to earn it, but it's oh so worth it.

The more fast-lane freedom you want, the more opportunities you'll be presented with, at higher and higher levels, to apply the principles covered throughout this book. You may have to forgive someone you never thought you'd forgive, because you realize forgiving them sets you free to soar. You might have to downshift your timetable on a goal because your need for speed is sucking the thrill right out of the pursuit.

The testing can feel awkward. It can feel challenging. You may question whether your right direction is right after all. But in rising to each challenge without regressing to old "wrong direction" ways, the tests will get easier and easier, not because the tests themselves are easier, but because you are better. And because you are better, you'll be rewarded with greater joy, greater fulfillment and, yes, greater success—success that feels richer than ever before. I am no exception to the tests.

You see, when it came to writing the last chapter of this book, I froze. For nearly two months, I actually couldn't pen a phrase. I can't tell you how many times I had this exact conversation with someone.

Them: When will you finish the book?

Me: I'm on the last chapter.

Them: You've been on the last chapter for a while now.

Me: Mind your business.

People who know me will attest that I'm very tactful and diplomatic in conversation, so however I pieced those last words together, they were dipped in honey so as not to offend. But the essence of my response nonetheless conveyed, "Mind your own business."

In that season of my life, I was experiencing some massive earthquakes (to say the least) in my business. When I started writing this book, I had been in a loving relationship for some time. Several months into writing the book, that relationship ended. I was half-packed and had already started garage selling, all in anticipation of a cross-country move on the road to what might be marriage.

To say the thrill was gone would be an understatement. How in the world could I write about "fast lane, right direction" when my lane looked as if it was undergoing some major reconstruction? Wasn't I supposed to have arrived? Isn't "right direction" about having it all together?

Sure it is.

It was during an old college mate's visit that the bigger picture, and the real purpose for this book, began to come together. Sitting on the floor in my living room, he asked, "So when will you finish the book?"

(You know where this is headed, right?)

I knew he meant well, so after pushing through the annoyance of having to verbalize what I already knew internally, I picked up the table of contents and pointed to two chapters in particular that explained why I was at an impasse in the writing. With all the setbacks going on in my life at that time, I was struggling with my identity, very much as we discussed in chapter 5. I was having a difficult time owning my authentic message as a speaker and was instead copying the blueprint of those who were at a level above where I aspired to be. Emulating effective strategies from other people is a good thing; losing your unique identity in the process—not so much.

At the same time, I was a poster child for the pursuit of perfection, and as we learned in chapter 8, there are few character traits more conducive to failure than the need for perfection. How could I have regressed back to that behavior and not even realize it was happening?

Has that ever happened to you? One minute you're cruising well above the speed limit. You're feeling good and you're "in control."

Job: *Check!*

Friends and family: *Check!*

Vacation: *Check!*

Promotion: *Check!*

Marriage: *Check!*

Kids: *Check!*

The next minute you're wrapped around a pole, so to speak... insecure, confused, frustrated, broken and wondering what the hell just happened, and more importantly, why hardly anybody noticed. This has happened to all of us before, and trust me, it will happen to you again. It's nothing personal—just a test.

As the identity and failure tests were happening to me, the voice in my head sneered, "Look at you. Your life is not perfect, so who are you to write a book about how to create a perfect life?" The taunting in my head was reinforced by that same college mate when he asked me the million-dollar question:

"So what do I get when I read your book?"

What do you mean?

"If I buy your book and follow what you say, will I finally 'arrive?' Are these the secrets to finally having it all, or what? Does my life ever get perfect?"

As he asked that question, it all became so much clearer for me. No more fog. Prior to writing this book, I thought I had cracked the "right direction" code. I had left my job, I had taken big risks, I was following my passion, so in many ways, I had cracked the code. But it was just a piece of the code. Those personal and business earthquakes challenged my beliefs in the midst of my right direction journey, and those tests forced me to grow to an even deeper understanding of how to apply these principles on a consistent basis.

When we are in right direction—our destination and mindset—even when we are in the midst of a rough road, we can still experience smooth sailing. Why? Because when you have a right-direction destination, the destination is authentic to you, and when the destination is authentic to you, it cannot fail. You might have to adjust your speed or metaphorically switch lanes here and there, but you always get back on track.

Secondly, when you have a right-direction mindset, you can do your part in pursuit of your destination, then confidently surrender how it all comes together, whether it happens in or out of your time frame, consistent or contrary to your plan. The better you get at managing your mindset and staying true to your authentic destination—in life, love, business or anything else—the faster you will cruise from one enriching experience to another, minus the undercover emotional drama so common to our fast-lane generation.

You know life is never going to be perfect. There's always something. The "10 Simple Steps" to accomplishing your wishes, goals and desires aren't so simple. As an achiever, you're wired to never feel as if you're there. But the great deception is that there's no "there" to get to. Author Carolyn Myss once said, "What you really want is to be madly in love with your life, and realize that everything you do counts."

"Right direction" is about being madly in love with your life. Isn't that what you want? I know it's what I want. In relationships, falling in love with the significant other is the easy part; staying in love with that person is a whole other matter, especially when the road gets rough.

So it is with right direction.

Most of us spend our lives chasing a feeling—a feeling of aliveness, hoping we'll find it in our job, our business, that marriage proposal or our kids. The challenge is that those magic moments are fleeting, and if we don't know how to sustain the moment, we're left chasing the next high that promises that...feeling.

But true fulfillment happens in between the moments, and if you're willing to make the choices outlined in this book, there's no end to the peace, vitality and purpose you can feel in between the milestones. Markus, the European entrepreneur we introduced in chapter 13, can attest:

"I wouldn't have my daughter Isabella if I hadn't made that choice. I wouldn't have this relationship where I feel so secure when I see my girlfriend; I just light up. I didn't have that in business. Here I have it every single moment. I have the joy of success, but just in another way. This is so much more."

So how do you get the "more" that Markus talks about? How do you bottle up the enthusiasm and hope of the brand-new "super you" before it gets knocked out by the bills, deadlines, insecurities and demands of the old you? It's pretty simple:

1.) Get Real About What's Real.

A good portion of *Fast Lane, Wrong Direction* focuses on you taking inventory of what's true about your life. Are you really unhealthy? Has your marriage dried up? Is your business not working out? Are you tolerating a situation you shouldn't? Are you taking charge of your career or letting your career take charge of you? Do your kids resent you because you don't spend enough time with them?

Oh, how skilled we've become at hiding from the truths, especially the ugly truths! You may have taken a hard look at areas of your life as you read this book, but if you want to maintain right direction beyond the final page, you must get used to telling the truth—the whole truth and nothing but the hardcore truth—about yourself on a regular basis. It's the start of real freedom.

2.) Find the Root.

The prior point reveals what is in your life; finding the root reveals who you *are* in your life. The latter is a crucial piece of information you need to know. Taking inventory of where you are personally or professionally is a huge part of the right direction formula, but what surfaces from that inventory are only symptoms of the problem; they are never the problem themselves.

In fact, many challenges that show up in your life are not necessarily problems at all. They are merely situations. How you contribute to or respond to those situations creates the problem. For instance, the reality that your marriage is stale is not a problem—it's a big, fat fact. That you have deprioritized your spouse relative to your work for the past two years… now that could be a problem. In actuality, that is your root.

Craig, a thriving investor, got this message loud and clear when he shared, "I now call my wife two or three times a day just to see how her day is going. Before, I would be too busy—in part because I wasn't 'getting' anything for it. Fast lane, wrong direction came from the workplace into my home. I was bringing the 'only the strong survive' mentality home instead of treating my wife as a delicate flower."

Remaining in right direction requires that you continually dig up your roots. Failing to do so puts you at the mercy of external circumstances for your happiness. You'll hear yourself saying, "If this changed, I'd be happy. If he or she just got it together, I'd be fine." Instead, dig up the roots and take full responsibility for your part in what's showing up in your life, business, marriage, parenting, etc., then use whatever strategies from this book that apply to you to correct your course.

That's when you'll sustain those magic moments on the way to your next milestone.

That's how you'll generate those feelings of aliveness on a regular basis. It's not what's outside of you that needs to change first. It always, always, always starts with you.

3.) Listen to Your Life.

Florence Scovel Shinn wrote, "Many people are in ignorance of their true destinies and are striving for things and situations which do not belong to them, and would only bring failure and dissatisfaction if attained."

If you want to maintain right direction in your life, try minding your own business. If you are overly concerned about aligning your choices to other people's, you have no hope of remaining right direction. You may find your right path only to deviate from it because it doesn't look like everyone else's.

When you take inventory of your life, it will be hard to distinguish between what is real and what is an unfair comparison to other people's situations if you fail to account for your personal path. What you perceive to be a problem may not be a problem at all. In fact, it might be the perfect circumstance for your life when it eventually plays out, but you won't have the foresight to recognize it.

Keep in mind that right direction is not a universal destination. What is right for someone else may be the complete opposite for you. So as you begin applying these principles to your life, ensure that the canvas on which you are painting is your design, not the next man's blueprint.

Give it Away

Many of us fail to recognize that life is meant to be given away—all our love, laughter and talent—such that at the end of our lives we've used it all. All too often we spend our time preserving our life, hoarding our toys, guarding our hearts, protecting ourselves from failure and rejection, and thereby missing out on the magic of truly living. It's because we don't know that our life is richly and lovingly guided. We think it is, we certainly hope it is, but we don't know it is.

> "It was just like therapy. It was wonderful, and I think that's the first time I really experienced having something as my day job that was very much aligned to what I believed as a person. I think the people who feel like their work is a calling (like clergy)... this was probably something like what they feel. It's the feeling that what I'm doing as my vocation is also my avocation."
> —Erika Watson, founder of the Washington, D.C., Chapter of Dress for Success

Like Erika, when you get that your life is bigger than you, your fears and your ego trip, you'll grasp that accepting "fast lane, wrong direction" is no longer an option. There are too many people who will benefit from you becoming the very best version of yourself. When you alone become enough, you'll constantly step up to give away more of the best of yourself, instead of stepping up for yet another validation that you're worth something.

Perfection is no longer your ever-elusive goal; you get to give that away. You get to give away comparing yourself and your progress to the next person because you realize there's never ever a comparison. You give away your fear of criticism because you're strong enough to incorporate the objective feedback and discard the rest. Your success is no longer up for debate because it's no longer about you; it's bigger than you, and it cannot fail. Your very life, at whatever stage of growth you happen to be, is an answered prayer to your husband, your wife, your kids, your co-workers, your customers, your classmates, your boss, even the stranger on the bus. Is right direction still hard and scary and cloudy at times? Abso-freakin-lutely! But you're well familiar with hard and scary and cloudy.

It is true that sometimes you will find yourself in the fast lane going in the wrong direction—in your career, business, even with the love of your life. In those moments, the last thing you need is motivation to do more of the same. In those moments… it's time to stop, look and listen to your life.

Slow down so you can speed up.

Acknowledgments
It Really Does Take a Village…

There's an old adage that says, "It takes a village to raise a child." I wholeheartedly agree with that statement, but I tell you this—it takes another one of those villages to publish a daggone book!

To say I am humbled to my core by the countless people all over the world who played a role in this remarkable project would be a colossal understatement. I could not have possibly penned this work without the expertise, guidance, encouragement and extraordinary insights of every person mentioned below. I pray each of you recognizes just how much your contribution matters, not only to me, but to the countless people who will be inspired by this work for years to come:

Dennis Tuttle—To the world you are an outstanding editor; to me, you will forever be "King Tut." Words cannot express how grateful I am for your guidance, coaching and expertise. Your belief in me and this project was evident, and I thank you for literally willing me across the finish line.

Rosemary Tran Lauer—You are my "Oracle" and I am immensely thankful for your friendship, your wisdom and your heart of goal. You inspire me to love bigger.

Lekisha Middleton and Kerry-Ann Powell—God placed you in my life for "just a time as this." Thank you for supplying a gazillion laughs, insights and big dreams throughout the course of this project! Sometimes, I needed them more than you knew.

Stacey Martino and Stacy Kennedy—You are two of the most encouraging women to ever walk the planet! At just the right time, your cheerful words gave life to my spirit, allowing me to give life to others. Never underestimate that gift.

Brenda Bertrand —You were there in the beginning, brainstorming titles and subtitles for a book with no form and no content. Look at it now!

Lene Fich—You reviewed the very first draft during your round-the-world trip and encouraged me to take all the time I need to "finish strong." Best advice ever.

James Malinchak—I started with talent, heart and a message I didn't even know I had. You provided me with the positioning and skill to make it meaningful. Thank you for sharing your knowledge of marketing, success and equipping that so many of us share our messages with the world.

Deann Raleigh and Leslie Bray Brewer—Proofreaders extraordinaire. Your third-party review of the manuscript was invaluable. This project would not be what it is without your input.

And to all my contributors, whose candid, funny, vulnerable sharing of their lives and expertise made this book more than I ever imagined. Thank you!

Nikki Barnett
Delise Bernard
Tricia Brennan
Kathy Brooks
Julie Marie Carrier
Joey Coleman
Lisa Brodie Cole
Julia Cronin
Johnny Lee Davis
Carla Douglin
Janine Driver
Lene Fich
Christine Temple Gaspar
Vanessa George
Libby Gill
Gil Giro
Clay Goldsborough
Vanessa Ferreira Halloum
Vicki Irvin
Jose Jimenez
Candice Jones
Finiana Joseph
Kim Kampp
Kimberly Keyton

Nathan King
Courtney Lake
Aubrey Layne
Jackie Lewis
Eric Logan
Mark McNeill
Andrea Moore
Tashena Middleton
Greg Newbold
Elizabeth Natasha Ngonzi
India Pinkney
Reyhan Reid
Damon Roberts
Selange Roberts
Garth Sandiford
Ruth Simwanza
Lauren Solomon
Michelle Thomas
Jennifer Tito
Adoara Udoji
Erika Watson
Rhonda Whitley
Leslie Woods

If I have forgotten anyone, please charge it to my head and not my heart!

—*Renessa*

About the Author and Speaker

Renessa Boley is best known as America's Premier Life Designer, equipping clients to succeed wildly in both work and life. Her skill set ranges from career coaching to keynote speaking and training for corporate and university audiences. Interwoven with her strategies of career management are the principles of strategic life design and peak performance, which together foster effective leadership, fulfillment and promotion in the workplace.

Renessa is a dynamic speaker and has appeared as a leading authority on ABC, CBS, NBC and Fox television affiliates across the country. She has also been featured in publications such as Career Builder, CNN.com, *Heart & Soul* magazine and *Washington Post*.

She invites readers to email her on info@renessaspeaks.com and visit her website at www.renessaspeaks.com.

> "Renessa simply dazzles! She's a huge value-add to any audience. I highly recommend her."
>
> —Terrence Noonan, 5-Time Emmy Award-winning producer

Renessa is available as a keynote speaker on:
- Life and Career Design
- Career Development and Promotion
- Leadership and Team Building
- Strategic Networking and Influence
- Transition to Entrepreneurship
- Success: From College to the Real World
- Performance, Productivity and Professional Presence

To schedule Renessa to speak at your next event:
Visit: www.renessapeaks.com
Email: info@renessaspeaks.com
Phone: 866-306-5241

Made in the USA
Charleston, SC
02 April 2014